UNITED STATES of GRACE

UNITED STATES *of* GRACE

**A Memoir of Homelessness,
Addiction, Incarceration,
and Hope**

LENNY DUNCAN

BROADLEAF BOOKS
MINNEAPOLIS

UNITED STATES OF GRACE

A Memoir of Homelessness, Addiction, Incarceration,
and Hope

Cover design: LoveArts

Print ISBN: 978-1-5064-6406-0
eBook ISBN: 978-1-5064-6407-7
Printed in Canada

To my daughter, Jenna. Bear, your sacred story will burn down empires someday.

CONTENTS

PREFACE

The Trajectory of Grace

Whenever I tell my story—how I grew up in West Philadelphia, left home at the age of thirteen, lived on the streets doing sex work and dealing drugs, got my GED in prison, and somehow wound up a preacher—I describe my life as a trajectory of grace. In fact, I think grace runs through the ley lines and county borders that litter the landscape of this country, churning through small towns and major cities. Our lives are a blind date with mercy, but we have to pay attention to see this grace revealed. The search for grace seems like a contradiction, to be very honest with you. How do you find a thing, a force, a powerful river of love whose currents sweep us away, usually from behind? But grace can be found, and we can wrap our arms around it and ride it to destinations unclear, unknown, and lovely. That's what this book is about, tracking this path of grace, stalking it down the highways that are crisscrossing this country like veins pumping the lifeblood of this nation throughout its holy, broken, and often misunderstood body.

An old Buddhist proverb describes a group of blind men who come upon an elephant for the first time. They heard that a strange animal called an elephant had been brought to the town, but none of them were aware of its shape or form. Out of curiosity, they said, "We must inspect and know it by touch, of which we are capable." So they sought it out, and when they found it, they groped about it. The first person, whose hand landed on the trunk, said, "This being is like a thick snake." To another one, whose hand reached its ear, it seemed like a kind of fan. Another person, whose hand was upon its leg, said the elephant was a pillar, like a tree trunk. The blind man who placed his hand upon its side said the elephant was "a wall." Another who felt its tail described it as a rope. The last felt its tusk and stated the elephant was hard, smooth, and like a spear.

Trying to capture the full beauty and majesty of the United States of America is like this proverb. How do I hold in tension the theft of the Rockies from Indigenous peoples with the beauty of the rising dawn over the Front Range of Colorado? How do I walk through the green rolling fields of North Carolina and not think about my great-great-great-great-grandfather and how he bled in those same fields, how the sweat of his brow is the very foundation of that state? How do I stand in New York City, walk the busy sidewalks of Manhattan, swept up in the awe of the great big things we are capable of, and ignore the NYCHA housing that is crammed next to the monuments to end-stage capitalism? That's the problem when we talk about America. We are grabbing the trunk and saying this feels like systemic racism, or grabbing the tail and saying this feels safe and like home, or rubbing the ear and saying this feels smooth and just. None of us, including our leaders, has a full picture. I'm certainly not claiming to have a full picture. But I have seen this country's highways and byways up close and personal. I have seen more of it than almost everyone I know. I'm going to tell you a secret that most people who know me or have read my previous work would never guess:

I'm in love with this country.

I mean in a passionate, up-all-night-texting love affair. Kissing-when-no-one-is-looking-because-it-feels-so-new love. Like sweaty-palm-hand-holding-down-the-streets-of-Brooklyn kind of love. I mean singing-love-songs-while-cracking-open-the-fire-hydrant-for-the-kids-down-the-street kind of love.

This is a book of contradictions. I will be telling you about a world that has done nothing but reject, try to kill, or push aside everything that I am. I will be telling you about the hope I have in the gathering of communities across a large swath of the North American continent. Places and communities that have given us evidence, both historically and more pointedly lately, that we shouldn't have hope in them. That we are irredeemable. Permanently shattered and thus unsalvageable. And perhaps this is true; it certainly feels that way as I scan the morning news or see anything coming out of Washington, DC. I get the sense that this is what it feels like when great empires fall on their face. The pain and tragedy and utter senselessness of it all are too much for any of us to bear on most days. This book won't deny any of this. In fact, the plan is to embrace all your tears and scars and very rightful reasons to take this American dream to task. But I want to suggest that the power of this place is its people and not its institutions. In fact, when I talk about America, I do so with the underlying assumption that its institutions are evil and corrupt. Full stop. But the dreamers—those of us still engaged in building and often rebuilding the promises and vision of this country, those of us who are wrestling with the angels and will likely walk away like Jacob, limping but blessed—we are America.

We are the America that I'm writing about. That I'm in love with. That I want to tap on the shoulder and remind that I'm still here. You are still here. That can never be stolen from you. That same great-great-great-great-grandfather I told you about, his son fought with the Union army for this thing that was always denied—freedom. That veteran had a son after he moved back to North Carolina, and his family grew to span the length of the entire East Coast. Thirteen children of a Union army vet, brothers and sisters, one of whom settled in West Philadelphia—my grandfather. He went to fight fascism and the Axis but returned to a country that denied him benefits and the dignity of being treated like a man. Yet he carved out a life for us all on Sixty-Third and Race in West Philadelphia. The same block where I watched someone open a fire hydrant on a summer day to break the ninety-degree heat, creating my first Black hero at four years old, the older kid who dressed so damn cool and had the key to open up the "water plug," as I called it, and create joy in what some would characterize as a joyless place. Three feet of wet, hot concrete joy and barefoot jubilation. That's the spot I'm trying to hit in this book. What I'm aiming for. What I will most likely miss.

I'm going to tell you about my life and the country I love through a series of tragedies and stories that are deeply personal, are filled with pain and struggle, and might actually horrify some of you. It will be a vast array of trauma and things no one should have to go through. It is in these really broken places that I will try to tell you about love and grace.

I'm afraid. I'm afraid you will misunderstand me or think I am trying to paint a rosy picture around the stark industrial wasteland that is this country. I am afraid. I'm afraid that when I give you almost all of me that I can stand that you will weigh me and find me wanting of the things that you have come here for. That you will see me plant gorgeous, vibrant living things next to death and white supremacy in the same paragraph—the same sentence, even—and think that I don't see the paradox or the utter ridiculousness that is my hope for you. For us. For myself. For this country. For these things that many would have you believe you don't deserve to hope for anymore. I am afraid that if you are white, you will walk away saying this isn't the America I know, and if you are Black, you will say this damn fool still believes in our lives. I am afraid. That if you are a person of color, you will feel left out of my narrative. I am afraid. That if you are queer in this country, you may wonder why I am comparing our incredibly glorious way of loving each other and the world to heteronormative paradigms that only seem to bring misery to us. That you will wonder why I keep setting the bar at what a heteronormative society has deemed as love even though we know it is a whitewashed tomb bereft of the hope of resurrection. I am afraid.

I'm so damn tired of being afraid, and I'm willing to bet you are too. I'm willing to gamble on the fact that you are tired of hiding in the shadows and the ambiguity of grace. That you are tired of being wedged between mercy and despair. We are all sick of the actual magnificence of this country being obscured by monstrous leaders who are jerking off to fever dreams about nationalism. We are all over the tired narrative that nothing is "woke" enough, which leads to the oppression Olympics, where no definable change actually happens because we are too busy policing one another while the riot police teargas our neighbors. I'm tired of the narrative that there is nothing of worth in this place I live, and love, and breathe in.

I'm tired of being afraid to say that grace is real and it's real for this country. I'm tired of feeling like my belief will be dashed against the rocks of iniquity moments after it dares to be reborn. And we know what this fear is. This mounting evil slowly but surely marching from the beaches of Atlantic City to Five Points in Atlanta. That is interjecting itself into conversations in Des Moines and rising like floodwaters in Houston. We already know what this evil is, and we know it isn't the people. Our fate isn't different than that of others who were brought here as cargo. We are the story of our Indigenous siblings, whose home was destroyed by our very presence. We are the scared eighteen-year-old kid who isn't so much storming the beaches of Normandy as being thrown out of a boat into a greater battle well beyond his capability to truly grasp. We are a scared little Black girl walking into a school surrounded by National Guard troops for the crime of wanting to learn.

We are amazing. Even when the story of this country isn't.

I would suggest that it is the responsibility of every generation to carry on this never-ending battle for freedom. But more importantly, it's our job to capture the story of each of us and treat those stories as sacred. Here and now, we get to write the scripture of the future. It may not get into the canon, but we can't deny that stories have a way of speaking to us in the deep, hidden inner recesses of our souls.

My story can only be my own, but by placing myself in the grand mural God is painting on this country and not attempting to hide its more violent hues, I hope to create space for you to find yourself in my story. To track the distance between us so that whether your own story sits right up against mine or there is a gulf of difference, somehow knowing where I stand, my location, makes us both feel less alone. Real connection through pages spread over the distance of months or years to publication. A note in a bottle sent over rivers of love and grace that hopefully wash up on your shores. A direct map to my heart. Or as Mos Def (Yasiin Bey) put it, "From wherever I am to wherever you are." We are dying for real connection and authenticity. So for me, this is my attempt to be as naked as possible in a room full of strangers.

I propose to you that grace is the only export and commodity that this country has left that isn't tainted by a history of systemic oppression that has gripped this nation by its throat. That the gullible hope they sell you in elementary school isn't something to be completely ignored or cast off. That somewhere between the propaganda and the foolish dreams is the flesh and bones of a country that we know and love.

We will follow the trajectory of grace as it bounces around our bodies like a bullet.

1

GOD FOUND ME AT THE BACK OF A GRATEFUL DEAD SHOW

I stood in the back of Hampton Coliseum on the edges of the crowd. It was February 12, 2010; I was thirty-one years old; and it seemed like the music playing from the band was the deep, painful groans of twenty years of pain and loss being laid out for the whole world to see. Each note pierced a place deep inside, and as the crowd moved and shifted as one mass of humanity crying out, I was in rhythm not only with them but with the world. I first experienced this feeling of connectedness at a Grateful Dead show many years ago, so it was fitting to finally feel it again here. As the band started to close the show, it felt like an era was closing for me.

There's nothing like a Grateful Dead show. Imagine, if you will, a circus and a carnival wrapped into one giant Day-Glo package. People following a band around the country because for some reason they have tapped into the collective consciousness of the American experience—for several generations, at this point. Scraping gas money together by selling T-shirts, psychedelics, crystals, carpets, pants, shorts, food delicacies from various cultures, pipes, art, prints, beers, waters, and sometimes pieces of their very souls to get to the next show.

A caravan of misfits whose only uniting theme is a band most people don't think is touring anymore. These are explicitly white spaces—I was often the only Black person around this scene. Dozens of bands are doing this thing, from Phish, to Widespread Panic, to JRAD, and each one of these separate scenes interlocks to create the underground of American culture that kept me alive when I was homeless and thirteen years old with nowhere to go in America. More about that later.

On that night in February 2010, things had just fallen apart for me again. About forty days prior, I had been sober for over a year, edging toward two years. It was the longest period of sobriety I had ever had, and I thought I was finally turning some sort of corner in my life. That I had somehow discovered the magic place where I could be the impossible: happy and sober. At the same time and in the same place. But I was wrong, and here I was at the edge of the crowd, rehashing a world I thought I had left and had somehow grown beyond. It was the worst forty days of my life. I had been drinking again, and I have never felt so defeated by booze. I was going to die like this, and I had lost the will to fight.

There on the edges of the crowd, as the band played on and the mass of people pulsated with the rhythms and the rising of the guitar, I was about to hit the end of my life as I knew it. When I woke up from a blackout, I was on a bus leaving Philadelphia heading to Key West. A faceless companion by my side. She was a real person, of course, with a family and friends and a life, and I had convinced her to come along with me. I had my first drink a few nights before, and almost instantly, my roommates wanted me out. What led me to that first drink I'm not sure I can explain. A friend once told me that if I wanted to stay sober for good, I would have to build the kind of life that's worth not throwing away. I hadn't done that. I had never evolved past the point of a trivial job and making meetings. I'm not trying to take away from the power of twelve-step programs, but they aren't enough on their own. Most people in this world wither without a life of deep meaning. We turn inward, and without some richer source—divine or otherwise—to tap into, we spiral toward our worst instincts. Maybe for you that's anger or depression or a thousand other death-dealing things. For me it was and probably always will be booze: self-destruction by way of full-body immersion in whiskey. Maybe it's my childhood or this country's treatment of me. Maybe it's prison's long-term effect on me. But my life has often felt as though it was made of tissue and could be easily swept away by forces beyond my control.

The only way I thought I could regain control was to do the destroying myself. I waited a few days for my next paycheck and hopped on the next bus out of town. My friend Davester was in Key West, seemingly having a great time on his annual trip to the Keys, and somewhere in between slamming some coke and doing a few shots of Maker's Mark, I decided I would too. My faceless friend's family convinced her to turn around the day after we arrived, and I started floating around Duval Street, hanging on Davester's coattails. Within a week, I couldn't sleep past 6 a.m. without the rock-and-roll shakes of DTs (delirium tremens) waking me up like a cruel master barking the orders for the day. I would guzzle a pint so damn quick and stagger to the little job I had landed. I worked at one of the booths that enticed tourists to go paragliding or on a booze cruise. As part of the gig, I had three weeks to do everything we offered at the booth. Which meant that many days—after I'd drunk at least a fifth before noon—I would close the shop at 3 p.m. and go diving, or party on a booze cruise, or take out a Jet Ski. I'm sure it looked like I was having the time of my life, but alcoholism has a way of living so seamlessly next to life in this country, we often don't notice it.

This is what rock bottom looked like for me. I had eaten out of trash cans. Slept by the side of the road. Been sexually assaulted. Nearly died several times in different ways. But something about being in paradise and not being able to enjoy it even though I had the whole island at my disposal was soul crushing to me. It was like I was watching a series of still photos of the world having fun around me. I could touch the image, but I couldn't engage or enter the picture myself. The world was flat and had no depth. It was like a fly passing in front of my nose I couldn't grab onto or hold.

Life was happening all around me, but I couldn't live it no matter how hard I tried. I stood at the southernmost point in Key West one night at sunset. It's a thing you are supposed to do in Key West: watch the sun slowly fall below the horizon as orange and crimson bands of light shoot across the surface of the water until they melt into a soft pink. This is the kind of shit that can pull tears from the most hard-hearted person. I stood there muttering to myself, probably a quiet litany of why my world was crashing in on itself, while the woman next to me took in the view with a sense of awe I could barely engage with. She looked me in the eyes and said, "Hunny, smile. This is heavenly." I looked right back into her eyes, full of the sunset; said, "Lady, this is hell"; and turned around and walked away.

I was in hell when we wandered to Miami to follow the Grateful Dead tour—well, the closest thing left to Grateful Dead in 2010: a band called Furthur consisting of two original members and a few younger cats that brought new life and energy to the thing. The fact that this thing I loved seemed to be back and in full force since the death of Jerry Garcia didn't move me at all. None of that mattered, I realized. Music had been my only consistent companion since I was twelve. It was the only thing I would allow to whisper into the secret places of my heart. To soothe years of trauma and pain. I loved music deeply, and I would go to incredible lengths to experience it live. By the end of the first show, I knew that the music wouldn't be enough this time—it was barely making a dent into the morass of bitterness soaked in alcohol and despair. I half-heartedly tried to earn gas money and ride most of the tour, but even with free tickets from a friend who had to leave early, I wasn't sure I'd make it.

But there I was in Hampton, Virginia, half a dozen shows later. I'd made it into the cold Northeast, riding with some kid probably half my age who was already sick of the hard-luck case he picked up and seeing shadows crawl and writhe around out of the corner of my eye when I didn't have enough booze in me. I stood at the edge of the crowd, and I could tell the show was winding down. Phil Lesh, the bassist, had come out to do what was commonly called the "donor rap." Every night, Phil encouraged members of the audience to become organ donors. He had contracted hepatitis C before anyone really had a handle on it and ran his liver to the ground. He talked about Cody, a kid who decided to be a donor and, through his act of kindness, saved five people, including Phil. I'd been to enough shows by now to know that this donor speech always came just before the encore song. I edged farther out beyond the crowd, where the lights barely illuminated anything.

The band started to sing a song called "And We Bid You Good Night," a soulful a capella arrangement based on an existing folk song.

The lyrics open with, "Lay down my dear brothers, lay down and take your rest / Oh won't you lay your head upon your savior's breast / I love you, oh but Jesus loves you the best / And I bid you goodnight, goodnight, goodnight."

I stood rocking back and forth to this tune, and I knew it was over. The battle that had been raging inside me for over twenty years was coming to an end. I knew that either I was going to be dead by the morning or something was going to happen. In response to the lyrics, the crowd clapped in unison to keep time with the band. It was about as intimate as ten thousand people can get.

That's when I heard it. A voice. From deep down inside, this voice was so quiet, I could hear it over a crowd. A voice so quiet, it could level mountains. A voice so quiet, it could stop a riot. A voice so quiet, it makes the world stand still. The voice of the divine doesn't scream truth; it *is* truth, and when it enters your life, all other things stop. You listen. And you are changed. Its message was simple and clear.

You are getting sober today.

I felt the weight of decades suddenly slide into place with a satisfying click, like a key that's been stuck in the lock but finally turns and opens the door. I felt myself inwardly rearranged almost instantly. The most amazing thing about this voice is that I believed it. Hearing a divine voice may strike you as strange or outside your experience of this world. Let me be clear: it was completely outside mine too. But think of the chorus of voices you hear every day, the constant narrative we call our minds. I was hearing a lot of voices leading up to this. Their messages were "Kill yourself," "You are worthless," and "Who could ever love you?" But this voice outside the usual stream of consciousness, it spoke with a quiet, assured authority unlike anything I had ever heard before and ever since. It was like a voice over a raging sea that called my name.

I immediately associated the voice with Jesus Christ of Nazareth. I was about as near a Christian at this point in my life as our justice system is equitable, meaning not at all. My first thought was, *What the fuck?* But I knew. I knew right then and there it was Jesus. I can look back and see that it was God's grace completely unmerited and frankly unwanted entering my life the way an invading force of mercy often does: it is overwhelming and all-encompassing. No matter what your experience has told you up until this point and what evidence you have that God doesn't care for you, your doubts will be immediately thrown on the bonfire of this new thing whose flames are slowly burning away your impenetrable walls of reason.

I had all the reasons in the world to believe the exact opposite of what this voice was telling me. I had no chance of getting sober. Jesus may have been a historical figure, but he wasn't any sort of divine being, and he certainly didn't speak to people here and now. But instead, I was sure of two things: I was getting sober, and I had just heard Jesus Christ of Nazareth.

My surroundings suddenly snapped back into focus, and I heard the lyrics rise up from the band again: "I'm walking in Jerusalem just like John (bid you goodnight, goodnight) / Walking in the valley of the shadow of death (bid you goodnight, goodnight, goodnight)."

It was like the prophets and the saints were singing over my scarred soul, sending their melody to me from the other side of the river of life. They pulled me to a place I had never been before: peace and direction.

I walked away before the song ended, gave my ride the rest of my tickets for the tour, grabbed my meager belongings, and left. Someone asked where I was headed, and I said out of nowhere, "The hospital." As I walked out, a light dusting of snow started to fall. I made my way up the nearest highway on-ramp to find the local hospital. I was moving along with steps that weren't my own, and I had a sense of peace and contentment that I hadn't had in a long time.

As the flakes fell, it seemed that all the world was pausing, holding its breath for my next move. It was my last time hitchhiking, although I didn't know it at the time. I stuck out my thumb as I walked down the highway determined—but for what, I didn't know.

This book is my love letter to America. As a queer Black man, I have often been cut off from and rejected by America and denied the true sense of promise in this country. I have never been treated like a citizen deserving of all the rights and privileges owed to Americans. America as a system has often felt more like an adversary than a friend. It has felt like a weight on my back and the scars on my face as I smile up at a God who is beyond any understanding. The concept of America, the American dream, I think is often a moving target—constantly being shaped and evolving into something this society is going to either fall short of at best or trample and spit upon at worst. Our institutions and leaders have fallen short of the American vision. In fact, they are so focused on holding on to power that they lack the ability and, dare I say, love to even see that vision anymore.

And yet my story is profoundly American. It just won't look like the America that most of you, my readers, know. I'm sure I will fall short of capturing *your* America. In fact, if that's what you are looking for, see if you can get a refund right now. If you are a white cis male, this probably goes doubly for you.

Groundbreaking Black theologian Dr. James Cone gave a talk a few years before his death. During the Q-and-A period, a white man raised his hand and said that the struggle for Black liberation was basically over. That the '60s and civil rights movement had moved the needle so far forward—almost to equity—that the time had come to end the conversation. He accused Dr. Cone of being the one who was stirring up racial animus. Dr. Cone listened quietly, intently. He paused to ponder his response and then simply said, "Sir, we live in two different worlds."

That will be true for me and much of the readership of this book. In my previous work, I have tried to dismantle your world so you can deem mine real. In this book, I will not refute the existence of your world. But white America is something I only know through observation and from the terrorism it perpetrates in my life. Nevertheless, I don't dispute that the experience of white America is real. And so I ask for the same respect. I hope to paint such a rich picture of my life and experiences that you can through observation glean some firsthand experiences. Both the bad and the good.

We have an obsession with treating the margins of this country as if they are joyless places to be pitied and scorned, bereft of anything resembling love or God.

But the truth is, it is in the broken, shadow places, those cracks in between society where most of my generation fell, where the music swelled and the lost, forsaken, and disposed lived—it is there that I experienced the God that I know today. Somewhere in between here and there is where I spent most of my formative years. Running wild across the I-70 or the I-80. Screaming down the

1 on the coast. Sitting in the back of a Greyhound bus, where freedom often smelled like the blue waters of bus toilet and sweat.

These are the contradictions of my American experience. And I won't even be able to share them with you perfectly; I will have the timeline all fucked up because twenty years of drug use have only exacerbated what we already know to be true: all personal memory is unreliable. So this is *my narrative*, as best as I can share it with you. I will change the names of people because they didn't ask me to write this book. Much like the writers in Jesus's time, I'm not trying to give you an exact historicity. I'm trying to capture what these experiences meant to me and still mean to me. They were the forces that shaped me in the way that waves shape a shore. By beating it and chipping away at it. America, you have beaten me and chipped away at me until I was what you needed me to be. The way a forge takes solid metal and, in the moment of the highest temperatures and through white-hot flame, makes it malleable and liquid. It can be poured into a mold or shaped with a hammer. America, I often wonder if you are the mold that forms me or the hammer that beats me later.

America is the crucible, the forge, the hammer beating me out of shape. Or into a new shape. But the fire is all God. A fire that is untamable, that has been harnessed and misused but not conquered by the powers that be. God's mercy is the force that kept breath in my body as I tried to dash my life against the rocks. It's Resurrection.

Moments like that snowy day in Virginia, when the world conspired to drag me by my hair, kicking and screaming, toward life.

My life has followed a trajectory of grace: the specific route God used to reach me that was built through a series of actions and events piling up and creating a spiritual momentum that I couldn't avoid, duck, or hide from.

The truth is, nothing went perfectly to get me from where I was on February 12, 2010, to where I am today, sitting in a random coffee shop in Bed-Stuy, Brooklyn, putting my story down in words for you, a stranger.

I was picked up by an immigrant who barely spoke English. I knew enough Spanish to explain I was headed to the hospital. That I was sick. He barely understood me, but he knew I needed help. He took me to his home and woke up his wife so she could translate. I explained that I was an alcoholic looking to get to a hospital to get sober. That I was sorry I disturbed her. I remember her conveying my words and the look of sad realization in his eyes. He said something to her, and I gathered my things, expecting to be put out. Who the hell wants to help a stranger with something this big? *This scary.* She said he wanted me to stay the night and he would take me to a hospital in the morning if I still wanted to go. I was so struck by this invitation that tears welled up in my eyes. I gratefully passed out on the couch.

I woke up, and God was still real. At this particular moment, God was a five-year-old girl in a pink onesie with a plush bunny at her side, and God was staring me right in the eyes. I wasn't sure where I was, but it all flooded back to me. Including the powerful feeling that my life had a new direction. Her father smiled at her as he walked in, and they served me breakfast. My hand shook so bad, I couldn't get the eggs in my mouth. Who knows if I could hold it down. I was grateful for the gesture though. Being treated like a human when I had experienced so little of that in my life was utterly amazing.

After he finished breakfast—I couldn't finish mine— he took me to a store and was kind enough to let me buy two tallboys to keep the demons from crawling up the walls. It is my sad duty to report that my last drink was two tallboys of Sparks, the energy drink / malt liquor. After I slammed them down greedily, he dropped me off at the hospital.

That's America. That's the America I know. A Black queer kid sticks his thumb out in Virginia, and an immigrant takes him into his home, introduces him to his family, and then drives him to the rest of his life. This is what I want to show you.

2

WEST PHILADELPHIA BORN AND RAISED

I grew up on Sixty-Third Street. More precisely, between Sixty-Second and Sixty-Third on Race Street next to a Jamaican social club and disco. The Duncan house was nestled between our neighbors Butch and Ms. Muriel, Mr. Ernie's house, and the Jamaican club next to Mr. Ernie. Three little squat homes and a little social club. Down the street from Morrone's Water Ice and Pizza Plus. Seven blocks from Jim's Steaks. We can talk about the gallows humor of a writer who talks about race in America being born on Race Street someday if we ever meet, but I have some really fond memories of growing up on that little stretch of block between Sixty-Second and Felton Street. The houses were of course row homes, but not like the large monstrosities over on Chestnut Street. They were short, squat, and drab in a way that I don't think I can describe. In fact, the only one that stuck out was ours because my grandfather, Edward, worked so damn hard at it. My grandfather had thirteen brothers and sisters who had migrated north from North Carolina sometime in the first few decades of a new century, after the abolition of slavery. My great-great-great-grandfather, having served in the Union Army with a New York regiment, brought home stories of the North, and it seems to have become synonymous in the family lexicon with the freedom from oppression. *The North.*

By the time I was born, I represented the third generation of Duncans in Philadelphia. My grandfather had two boys and a girl, my father, Leonard, being the youngest. A World War II veteran who served in the Pacific Theater as a cook and a musician, he was denied access to the GI Bill. From the records I traced, he went to a VA hospital and applied for a housing loan, and it appears he was not approved. He rarely talked about the war, and while the rest of the family seemed to feel loved by Edward and his wife, Gertrude—or Gert, as she was called—my father always expressed never being loved enough. Have you ever seen a raw slab of meat fresh from the slaughterhouse or at a deli? Not in a chain store; no, I mean like a local deli. A carcass stripped bare, where you can see the nuances of muscle and veins. The contours of what makes up the insides of a living thing. The ugly redness of it all. That was my father's emotional state most of my life and, I suspect, throughout his childhood. His emotions were plain to see and often brutal to witness. They bled out into the daily lives of all those around him, and—like a carcass—he had the things that helped him function removed, weighed, and found wanting by a world that was stacked against him in a way that was beyond his reckoning. Leonard Alexander Duncan Sr. was my father. My first friend. My fallen hero and my main abuser growing up. He was a tragic story of the meat grinder of Black life in Philadelphia in the '50s and '60s. Born with what I would categorize as severe learning disabilities, he challenged my grandma in ways that I'm sure seemed beyond daunting to her. The legend goes that when he was three or four, he was fascinated by cars and would run out into the street after them to get a closer look. By the time he was an adolescent, he had been hit by cars multiple times. I can only guess at the lack of medical care he received at local hospitals. Due to the "social promotion" system in Philadelphia, he was thirteen or fourteen—almost in high school—before his teachers realized he couldn't read. Severe dyslexia and losing his left eye to a broken bottle during a fight scarred my father on several levels, not the least of which is somewhere deep down in his soul. He seemed always to feel unloved, uncentered, and hardly understood.

My mother was wild and, in my eyes, always holy. White, Irish, twinkling blue eyes, bright-red hair, and the same smirk I have in every picture you will ever see of me. She grew up in Hazelton, Pennsylvania, a small mountain town around one hundred miles from Philadelphia. She was trouble from the moment she was born. Loretta Mary Sweeney was the youngest of four. The daughter of a coal miner, she grew up in a house full of domestic abuse, drinking, and—in the way only people who grew up in homes like that will ever understand—strange love. Strange because the human will to configure and co-create love in the most broken situations is one of the great things the Creator has given us. My mother was born on Valentine's Day 1957 and could find love anywhere. I think that is the resilience of women. Her parents, John and Helen, were a strange pair. John Sweeney's family story intermingled with the Molly McGuires of local fame in those mountains. After finishing his shift at the coal mine, he would walk down to the Veterans of Foreign Wars (VFW) and sit with his buddies whom he served with almost every day, drink bourbon, and smoke Pall Malls or Lucky Strikes. He lived well into his seventies that way. Lighting up and slamming down. Helen was Greek Orthodox and was not well liked by John's family as a result.

My mom grabbed her acoustic guitar in the early '70s and was notorious for sticking her thumb out and trying to get as a far away as possible until someone from her large extended Irish family saw her and dragged her home or she called her aunt Sissy for bus fare home when whatever escapade she was on went off the rails. My uncle John—her brother—went to Vietnam. He wasn't drafted;

he enlisted to serve with Army intelligence. The story is he left as a young Republican and a "patriot," as my mom put it, and came back disillusioned and lost. Her sister Danielle, who grew up in the same home where they witnessed violence and saw their mother being hit by their father, had the opposite reaction than my mom. Some people in that situation use perfection as a survival tool. Some act out. Some strike out on their own. Another uncle whose name I don't even know sexually abused my mom. She was never clear on details, but I know that's the incident that started her urge to leave. Trauma. The code of silence in that generation was deafening, and in the Black community, for my father's family, doubly so.

Now, these stories were all told to me when I was very young. But suffice it to say, my parents weren't exactly the pairing either family had in mind.

I tell you all this because my family didn't happen in a vacuum, and these next parts are going to seem like I am piling on. But I think a life of grace and forgiveness comes from unearthing the past and trying to understand the generational chain of events that set your own life and story in motion. I'm sure that members of my family would tell you that the story they received may have been very different or they may have experienced it differently. Neither story is untrue. To my cousin Nicole, whom I love dearly, my father was her favorite uncle. He was always funny, loving, kind, and caring to her with a tenderness I never experienced. This is true for her and a touchstone of her life. To me, my father was a powder keg who could go off any minute, and the world was nothing but fire and sparks that threatened to light the tinder of our fragile lives. This is true for me and a touchstone of my life. The complexity of personhood is a thing of beauty and deep frustration for the world. By examining these stories, I've had to come to terms with the fact that assholes say and do good, sometimes even great and life-giving things. Can deeply flawed people sometimes write, preach, sing, create, paint, and manifest perfection? The answer I have landed on is yes. At the same time, those people we admire most can sometimes really let us down. The journey of understanding our history is often one of forgiveness.

But to be clear, this isn't a treatise on forgiveness or some call for you to forgive those who have abused you. If I was saying that, you would be well within your rights to tell me to get fucked.

Forgiveness was survival for me. You have to understand that I had crafted a narrative of righteous anger that engulfed me. One could even argue Holy Anger. And the truth is, it was justified. But it was still poison that was slowly eating me alive. But to live another day, I started to have to see my parents—my father, in particular—as a whole person. Created by a set of circumstances completely beyond their control and not simply a result of some of their shitty decisions. And even those decisions were likely a result of the stories they were told about themselves or had developed to survive.

It's hard to talk about where I grew up in West Philadelphia as if it were a monolith. In fact, it is hard to talk about anything in the Black community, which West Philly largely is, as a monolith. And it's just plain hard to talk about my childhood experiences and the systemic conditions that slowly squeezed me like a vice growing up. Looking back through the haze of the years and memories is a task that is often made more difficult by the range of the emotions or the trauma that is tied to a particular period. Not to mention the soul-crushing admission that we are often formed more by the most traumatic periods of our lives than by the most favorable. Add a little alcoholism and drug use in the '90s for spice and what you get is the gumbo that is the recounting of my own life. The fact that I am a storyteller is the garnish, if you will, or the plating. I struggle between frantically trying to capture the very essence of every moment of my life in a way that will make sense to the world and the realization that my story is just that—my story—and I can serve it out however I want. The latter because I just have developed a sense of utter defiance as a writer. I never want to give you what you want, how you want it. That feels like a trap of the industry at best and a prison at worse. The former because I still believe in the power of us seeing each other in our utter humanness. I still believe that sharing our stories can somehow bring us closer to tasting the divine. That through the sharing of the scrapes and scars, the bruises and the frustrations, the awkwardness that is this world sometimes, somehow we move the project that is America forward.

My parents met and fell in love in a drug rehab center in 1975. Both of their addictions had led them to a two-year residential program. Apparently, my mom hated my dad for the first year. Have you ever been to rehab? I highly recommend it. It is a world that, if used properly, can give one an entirely new North Star in life. The only entry requirement for this seemingly magical realignment of the soul is that you have to have burned your life to the ground. I mean, utterly and truly. It is only from that place that you can truly assess what work you have been called to do in this life. At least, if you are like me or my parents and have never been able to do that. To stop long enough and consider the way you are moving in the world. For Mom and Dad, this was their moment. As the story goes, on my mom's birthday—Valentine's Day— in 1975, she had earned her first weekend pass in a year. She wasn't a model citizen of this manufactured community apparently. But she'd finally earned a reprieve. She was going to drive her Volkswagen Bug to see her boyfriend, but he wasn't interested in this new Loretta. Clean and unable to party. He did what guys still do for some indiscernible reason to this day. He picked the worst time to cut a woman's heart to ribbons. He broke up with her via a payphone call, which is the '70s equivalent of ghosting or breaking up by text. My father found her crying in her VW and contemplating throwing it all away. He wanted to keep walking (he loathed her just as much as she loathed him). But something—call it the spirit, fate, destiny, or the first pangs of a conscience—stopped him in his tracks. He turned around; knocked on the window, which was fogged up from my mom's weeping; inhaled sharply; and said probably the most spiritual thing he had ever said up until that point in his life: "Are you OK?"

My mom relayed the sad tale of woe and how she was really thinking about just going out and getting hammered. My dad—in the second most spiritual moment in his life—canceled his plans for the day and took my mom to Atlantic City. They walked the beach, they talked, they eventually held hands, and by the time the sun set, they were in love. It's funny to think about that day in the parking lot of a Doylestown, Pennsylvania, treatment center. How my existence really only happened because of this strange little twist of fate. How there seems to be a possible reality where my dad didn't stop or didn't reach for her hand on the beach or where my mom told him to kiss her ass when he knocked on the window. Our lives are created out of fragile moments where the very trees hold their breath with anticipation to see what happens next, where the wind stops to listen in and the clouds pause to take a peek. This has always amazed and baffled me.

They were married six months after that day, much to the distress of both families. Although Pennsylvania repealed their miscegenation laws in 1780, the Loving case in Virginia was only eight years earlier, and many pastors and judges throughout the country would refuse to perform what was called at the time an "interracial marriage" by more polite members of society. You have to understand what a risky decision this was by both my parents. It was dangerous from my father's family's point of view. It was inviting confrontation from police and members of the Black community and would enrage whites when they saw them together. My mother's family reacted in the predictable way an Irish coal-mining family would be expected to. With racism and fear. I could be angry about this, about the effects of white supremacy and the way it separates the poor while we never keep our eye on those benefiting from the system. I could tell you harrowing tales I have received thirdhand about my grandfather's reaction. I could tell you that he once told my mom before she met my dad that she could go to a stadium full of brain surgeons and would come home with a hot dog vendor. Or the months of negotiations it took to gather everyone in my grandmother Gert's living room on Sixty-Second and Race for the wedding. I'd rather tell you about the photos I have seen from that day.

My dad with his Afro on full display and the absolutely awful tuxedo he wore, a brown-and-beige disaster. How my mom was wearing what appears to be a garter belt around her head in one photo and the look of joy as she laughed, her head tilted back, in the next. The cagey looks both sets of my grandparents had at the beginning

24

of the series of pictures and the twinkle in my grandfather Edward's eye later. How later, they are at the same table and all laughing. How we as people make joy at feasts. I can tell you how Jesus loves a wedding feast and a good party in general. I can tell you staring at these eight-by-ten glossies of distilled moments from the past that Jesus was at this particular party, even though he sensed the brokenness ahead for us as a family. I can tell you that Black joy is real. I can tell you that even Irish coal miners from the mountains can lay aside their racism for their daughter's happiness, even if it's only for a few hours at a time. I can tell you that two years later, everything changed.

I was born on the morning of June 30, 1978, at Doylestown Hospital in Pennsylvania. My parents were living outside of Philly at the time, near the rehab where they got sober. I don't know much from this time. It seems by all accounts, they were sober a few years and doing well, and then something happened. I have a newspaper article recounting how my dad was arrested for growing some pot—something that white America has now deemed profitable and acceptable in some areas. I'm not saying he was manufacturing and selling it. It was a few plants for himself. I don't judge my parents for what sobriety meant to them at the time. There were rehab centers in those days that let people drink as long as they stayed away from drugs. I think my mom was struggling with her sobriety too. Whatever happened, they had to get straight again. This was a constant drumbeat in our house. The endless cycle of sobriety, happiness, vicissitudes of life, using, chaos, crisis, sobriety, happiness, vicissitudes of life, ad nauseam.

What I do know is that something changed for Grandpa Sweeney, as I called him—or, more accurately, "Gran-a Sweenah." He raised me for a year. Here was this child that clearly wasn't white in his very white world that he loved dearly. You have to understand, whiteness is patrolled heavily by white people, whether they are conscious of it or not. They walk its borders, constantly looking for signs of invasion or impurity. They do this nowadays literally and figuratively, but back then in Hazelton, Pennsylvania, I was seen as coming from the enemy encampment. But he would pick me up first thing in the morning after my grandma got me dressed and let me toddle down the street with him to the VFW. He would proudly plop me on the bar and feed me cherries and let me drink soda. My fondest memories of being a very young child are these barely recognizable scenes of me in a bar, looking around at the jukebox and pool table. Old gritty dudes giving me nickels for some reason and the smell of whiskey on their breaths. Bars feel like home to me in a primal way. This will become important later, but it really fits the puzzle that is my story.

After a year in the mountains, whatever was wrong with my parents was "fixed," and we moved into the building on Sixty-Second and Race in the place above my father's parents' apartment. I called them Grandma and Grandpa Duncan, or more accurately, "Gran-a Doookun."

Daniel was born around this time—my little brother. Born with a nappy bright-blond fro and crystal-blue eyes, he was mischievous and funny. We couldn't have been more different. I was so silent as a toddler and baby that after six months, my mom took me to the doctor because I wouldn't cry when I was hungry or had a full diaper. Give me a toy and some room to play, and I would sit for hours in my own world, just sort of spaced out. The doctor assured her that everything was fine; she just had a really well-behaved baby. In fact, I never once acted out until the day they brought Danny home. The story goes that the whole family surrounded Danny when they brought him home. Holding him and kissing his chubby little legs. A swarm of cousins and aunts and uncles and grandparents. I stood in the corner by myself, glaring across the room with hatred. I was two years and two weeks old. Daniel was born on July 11, 1980, and was home by the thirteenth, my father's birthday. As I stood across the room, my mom held Danny out to me and asked, "Do you want to see your little brother?" I ran across the room and, at the fastest toddle I could muster, punched him in the stomach as hard as I could. They had to take him back to the hospital. He was fine, but still, what kid does that?

Danny was the exact opposite of me. My mother told me when I was in my twenties that I was the reason she had Danny, and Danny was the reason my dad had a vasectomy. He was colicky and loud. He also was mischievous, getting into everything. One time my grandfather Edward was tired of Danny getting into all the drawers of the house—I mean all of them—so he bought those early eighties-era child locks for the drawers. He came home from his job as an elevator operator and doorman in Downtown Philly and spent the whole evening drinking a six-pack of Schlitz beer and putting one on every drawer in the house. He started in the dining room and worked his way back to his bedroom. When he finished about two hours later, he walked to the kitchen and found that Danny had taken them all off, piled them all up, and was playing with them like action figures. Danny looked at my grandfather and fell over laughing. Once I got over the shock of having a young sibling, Danny was my hero as a kid. He naturally knew how to work a room and get whatever he wanted. If you have ever met me, you wouldn't believe this, but I spent most of my childhood awkwardly reading books and obsessing over human interaction, afraid to just be. Or talk to people. I felt alone and like an outsider almost from my first sentient thoughts. Danny had none of that angst or worry. He just *was*, and I found that amazing.

I can't capture the Black joy that was West Philadelphia in the early '80s. I have tried throughout my life. The soft pretzels and high socks. The Afros and the sound of the Stylistics playing from a record player. The endless pinochle games unfolding in the backyard under the constant haze of BBQ smoke and the smell of ribs on the grill as my uncles Eddie and Calvin argued over the method of cooking. The sound of a "water plug"—a fire hydrant for the uninitiated into the deep mysteries of Philadelphia—when it's first opened. The loud metal-on-metal grinding and the sudden release of the water as it starts to flood forth. The way it would bowl your little body over onto the hot asphalt and tar as you would tumble a little bit into bliss. The way the sprays of water would create rainbows in the air. The walks up the street to get a cherry-lemon water ice from Morrone's, which in my opinion was the undisputed king of water ice in Philadelphia. The music—I know I already mentioned this, but the soundtrack of our lives was intense. Ranging from Earth, Wind & Fire to Stevie Wonder to the occasional argument about whether Elton John counts as soul and playing "Bennie and the Jets" as exhibit A all night.

There was joy and happiness. There was love and laughter. And then there were the other nights.

I grew up in the kind of house where you knew what kind of night it would be by the way the keys hit the door. The way someone stumbled up the steps. As a child, I remember listening from my bed for the warning signs of violence. Was my father's stutter really pronounced? Could he answer questions? Was he still able to reason? Was my mom fed up with him and giving defiant answers that would end up with her lying on the floor bleeding?

Was tonight a playful night where I could wander out into the living room and charm my father until he fell asleep and my mom wouldn't get hit? Would I push it too far and get frustrated myself and say something that made my father feel small? Jealous of my intellect? This would happen when he would be really drunk and ask me to read something to him because he couldn't. I wasn't sure how much he could read when I was real young, and when I would ask probing questions about why he couldn't read the lyrics off the record, he would sometimes be so ashamed, he would lash out and slap me for talking down to him. The blows would fill my eyes with a deep red that would come from the corners and fill my line of vision until everything was jet black like the night sky. I would later learn that I was being knocked out. I would wake up on the ground confused but proud because I was the target and not my mom. But if I pushed it too far, she would try to defend me, and that would make it all so much worse. I would play these games late at night. Sometimes my grandfather would intervene. Other times the police would show up and make it worse. They would beat my father, then look at my mom with disgust and mutter "Nigger lover" under their breaths. The flashes of red and blue meant longer nights, where a sergeant would spend hours trying to convince my mom to press charges, but she knew what she knew. These weren't our friends or protectors. The way their eyes would cut through us as if we weren't really human would hit us in waves. You could taste the revulsion.

The cops would take my dad away for the night to sleep it off at the local station. My mom would pack our little bit of stuff and put me and Danny in the white Honda that had been through hell and back. We'd go to a place full of other mothers and kids in similar situations. My mom would get clear eyed and sober, and dignity would start to rise in her walk. She would start to really be happy. Those days I savored. Then one day, she would walk over to the payphone. A few days later, we would be back to the familiar drama of them both falling back in love again, and then back out of love. It all played out over and over again. Until it didn't.

This lasted until I was twelve. Everything changed when I had a God-given inspiration. Something deep down inside said, "Maybe you would be better off on your own."

3

BLACKNESS IS A REVELATION

Blackness. It is a state of being, consciousness, and heritage and can be an existential threat. It is something you are born into, and it can be a revelation. It can suddenly streak across the little world of a Black child in this country with crushing consequence and power. Blackness is beauty and glory. It is hushed whispers along riverbanks with the promise of freedom around the next bend. It is cousins who go to Jack and Jill of America and historically Black colleges and universities (HBCUs). It is Afro puffs and braiding and plaiting your sister's hair. It is berets and grease and wriggling little bodies who ain't trying to get their hair done. It is a siren call into a long line of ancestors and forbearers who watch you with love and concern. Blackness is the way you move and the way you talk. Or it isn't. It is what you call music and culture, or it isn't. It is everywhere and nowhere. It is the freedom to be and the ever-tightening noose around your neck. It is the first time you heard midnight marauders or the second time you went to a dance. It is a state of being that is policed and denied.

Blackness will yell at me online for trying to define it, and it will make up with me later at dinner next Sunday. It is the touchstone of my life and a weight on my shoulders. It is a forming part of my very personhood, but if you asked me what it was, I would be at a loss for words. Not because I don't have a lot to say, profess, sing, write, and proclaim about it but because it is massive and expansive in its life and history with horizons far beyond what any one of us can see. It is the plumb line of my story and the thread that binds my life together. It is who I am.

Blackness can be questioned. Put on trial. The questions start in the schoolyard and can last well into graduate school and beyond, in my experience. Blackness is policed by white supremacy, and sometimes those who have the deepest scars from this radical evil are themselves warped by it. *They start to police Blackness.* They start to play the same purity games of the oppressor. They dress it up in the righteousness of the "cause" and aim finely sharpened spears and swords at your most tender areas. They can poke and cajole you to act out and strike back. I have learned to not fight back against these folks; mostly, I weep for them, because they have been so damaged by evil that they live out these patterns.

Blackness can be painted into murals that would make the angels weep and make God pause the entire cosmos from expanding just for a moment to listen in to the deep brown, tan, caramel, and black colors sing their song. It can raise its voice to you and make you stop in your tracks to hear the words spoken by Blackness. Blackness can change the very nature of language. We communicate now with so much stolen Blackness that we don't even think twice about it as white America tells Blackness how dope it is. Blackness is sore knees and my grandfather's long bus rides home. It is the older cat on the corner who goes outside and washes, shines, and waxes his car to the sounds of the Delfonics every Saturday with religious reverence. It is a nod across a whitewashed room as you suck in your breath and prepare for the maelstrom of microaggressions and macrohatred that is this country right now.

Blackness is passing someone at work, and when they ask how it is going, you give them a deep, soulful look in the eyes and just reply "Man, you know" and keep walking, secure in the knowledge that they do. Blackness is the cold calculus of always carrying your ID with you, putting your wallet in the visor in your car so your hands can always be seen when reaching for it, telling your partner where you will be at all times, and driving like an old lady through parts unknown because statistically, the math ain't on your side.

Blackness is what I am. It is what I know. It is the waters of my baptism and the oil anointing my head. It is a source of incredible pride and shame all at once. It is the cry stuck in my throat and the tears I refuse to shed.

Blackness is glorious. Even in the United States.

My Blackness is not normative. I don't believe any-one's is. We share some commonalities and a sense of unity, but our experiences and reflections are all unique. I don't want to perpetuate racist tropes about the broken-ness of Black homes. *My family was the exception, not the rule.* We weren't the ones headed to church on Sundays or to Jumma on Fridays. We weren't the ones helping with the cleanup every other Saturday with the block captains, and we weren't the kids in the bounce house at the block party. College wasn't a goal but a wispy dream far away from my house. But every other family on almost every block I lived on was principled, loving, and full of life. Every group and community has that one family. *That one house.* I grew up in it. Blackness saved me in many ways. It gave me something to live up to, to take pride in, because I didn't get that at home. That was my family's failure, not my people's.

I was informed I was Black the way many young chil-dren are. With violence. We had moved to Maryland for some reason that I was unaware of. My parents had prob-ably pushed my grandfather into the familiar pattern of being way behind on rent and horrifying him with their level of violence and drug use. Crack cocaine had started its violent dance through West Philly and wasn't going to stop its routine for a while to come. It's funny to be seven or eight years old and know which drugs you'd prefer your parents to use. I preferred when my dad did heroin.

Less likely to be violent and easier to maneuver around. The euphoria he often felt was something that he would chase until the day he died. My mom I preferred with just the right mix of Wild Irish Rose and a small amount of cocaine. Enough to bring the redness out of her cheeks and give her energy to tell me stories. I inherited from her my entire sense of humor and wit and what I call my gallows irony. These were the toxic mixes and substance-laden landscapes of my early childhood. I was formed by midnight serenades of "Papa Was a Rollin' Stone" and jolted wide awake to teary renditions of Janis Joplin pining for a Mercedes-Benz. This was my cue to come out of my room and scan the scene. Would I have to intervene to stop a violent quarrel tonight or pantomime the cutesy-kid moves I learned from watching families on TV?

But all of this, of course, led to problems. Job losses or midnight moves. Barely remembered weeks living in a station wagon before moving into a YMCA in Harrisburg, Pennsylvania. Eventually, we ended up in Silver Spring, Maryland. I was always aware of race as a child. But in my case, it wasn't that *I* was different; it was that my mother was. She was often the only white person anywhere except for police, teachers, and folks I would see on TV. I would visit my grandparents, but that was like a visit to whiteness. My world was Black, and so Blackness was the norm. I knew my mother didn't fit and that I had to work harder to fit, but I could. The only whiteness I knew as a child was the fact that my mother was odd and the rest of her family didn't want anything to do with us because of our Blackness. She was the stranger in my childhood version of America, and I was the native. In my small patch of the dream deferred, I pitied her for not being Black and at times resented her for bringing my Blackness into question when I was playing outside.

Like many interracial or mixed couples of the time, my parents had started to drink the Kool-Aid as a toast to a postracial America. I would come home crying because someone made fun of me for my white mama, and they would sit me down and regale me with stories of the days to come when that wouldn't matter. That great people had sacrificed long and hard for their love and my very existence. That just a generation prior, their love was illegal in most states. That I would have been forced to eat at a separate table at a restaurant from my mother. That someone would have long ago killed my father for his transgression of being in a relationship with my mother. *That we were a miracle.* These talks were like scripture in my house. They were the sermons delivered in cathedrals of fleeting hope, and their cadence would rise and fall as they gave me the look pastors often give the flock, words that felt like dust on my tongue but delivered as if truer ones could not have been spoken. I was afraid to tell them that unlike my friends, I thought boys *and* girls were cute. Or that their words seemed untrue when compared to the world I was experiencing. To me, it seemed like race was more of an issue than the times and the stories they told. That it had gone underground somehow, this hatred, and had soaked every part of my world.

I thought the occasional rejection by my Black peers because of my white mother was the worst thing that could happen to me. From ages six to ten, any rejection feels like a heart breaker, a world killer, a cold knife in the back.

But nothing would prepare me for what whiteness had in store for me. Whiteness always recognizes something that is other. It is the nature of its very construction and raw materials. Drawn from the raw ore of four hundred years of colonialization and the oppression of Indigenous, brown, and Black folks, it was a ravenous predator stalking the periphery of my life. Stalking me as I tried to find my place in this country. Whiteness has been policed so well that it doesn't recognize its own heritage, except when that heritage offers even more privilege to whiteness.

It has created a culture, if one could call it that, built on capitalism, patriarchy, heteronormativity, militarism, and WASP visions of the future. It felt rejection in the '60s by its own children but came back with a vengeance.

In Silver Spring, it finally got to sink its claws in me and pronounce its judgment on me.

Nigger.

The first time I was called nigger was on the schoolyard in Silver Spring. I asked if I could join a group of kids, and they informed me they don't play with niggers.

I told my teacher and my parents. I don't remember anything happening except being labeled a "snitch nigger" the next day. The girls wouldn't come near me, the boys wouldn't play with me, and my teacher treated me and the few other Black kids in the class like prized pets. But the full consequences of whiteness would unfold in our apartment complex. My parents, I assume, were sober at this time or close to it. Our lives had dramatically improved, and this seesaw effect would be a hallmark of my childhood. Things were great, things were dangerous. Never anything in between. The apartment in Silver Spring was the nicest place I had ever lived. There was an elevator and a huge grassy field to play on with a creek behind it. My brother would get outside and take off at top speed. The freedom of playing and not being stuck in front of our steps like in West Philly was intoxicating. My father had an incredible fear because he was hit by cars as a child. Or at least, that's what my mom told us. The truth was he was abusive and wanted control of everything in his world. Including *his boys*.

Danny had developed the nickname "Hard Rock" in our house because he was just naturally defiant. His head, you see, was as hard as a rock. He walked to the beat of his own drum, sang his own tune. He took no shit from anyone. When he was in kindergarten, I was walking him back from the bus, and some kid called us poor because of our sneakers. Danny stopped dead in his tracks. I was on the verge of tears and just wanted to leave, mortified, sensitive, and not much of a fighter. Danny turned to face him, jumped a foot in the air, knocked the kid out with one punch, and then turned and walked away as if nothing happened, his Transformers backpack bouncing on his back.

One bright day after school, we raced outside to play and to just be boys. We soared out across the green field to our favorite spot just beyond where my dad could see us. Just over the crest of a little hill where the creek was, we could embrace the adolescent obsession with rocks and sticks and the creatures that lived in the waters of the creek. As we got over the hill and could look down, I felt a moment of panic. The cruel boys from the first floor were there. They eyed us with the typical disdain they always mustered up with the knowledge they had secured the best spot to play for the afternoon. At that age, despite all my talk of understanding the vices of the adult world, I was still very much a child. And I still saw the world through the eyes of a child. Imagination and possibility seemed endless, and I believed that every odd could be overcome. I knew monsters were real from my home life, but I also knew they could be slain. But not these two boys. They had waged a campaign of racist, hate-filled attacks on my brother and me since the day of our arrival to the apartment complex. I found hatred so confusing as a boy. Why did it exist and seem to twist people into knots? Why was it so unbridled and untamed, and why did it hold sway over so many? What most kids saw as fun or part of the weird rituals of adolescence, I recognized as an incredibly awful way to live. I remember reading *Lord of the Flies* as a kid and immediately recognizing that world as my own inner emotional landscape filled with the same horrors and fears.

The boys looked up at us; said, "Get your nigger ass outta here"; and started to throw rocks at us, peppering us with projectiles. I was a strange kid, reading everything from Sun Tzu's *The Art of War* to sermons from Martin Luther King Jr. I read about military strategy, and I knew, logically speaking, I had the high ground. So I picked a rock and hurled it down. It was a throw of horror and frustration at what I saw in the white eyes staring back up at me. My brother joined. Before long, I hit a bull's-eye, as it were, and I remember the instant fear when the rock hit our eldest tormenter's head. I saw him crumple to the ground as blood started to flow out of his head. The sheer panic. All I could think of was Piggy in *Lord of the Flies*, and I turned and ran at top speed back to the building. I wiped the tears hastily from my face as I pushed the elevator button frantically, and my brother brought up the rear, laughing the whole way. When we got inside, my mom asked us what was wrong. In the kind of unison that only the camaraderie of siblings ever seems to bring out of people, we replied, "Nothing." We both went to our room to await the eventual sentence from my father.

We waited for hours, but it didn't come. My father's punishment was often corporal in the extreme and at times abusive. He would sometimes beat us until we couldn't walk and, if he'd been drinking, punch us like we were grown men. But this day, it didn't come. We made it all the way to evening and breathed a sigh of relief.

We sat for dinner, cruel bullies defeated and no repercussions.

Then the knock came on the door. It is a strange day when whiteness makes its pronouncement on you. But when that day comes, when you realize as a small Black child that you are truly Black, well, all of us remember it. That's why so many writers talk about this day in their own lives. When Blackness is a revelation, and a pale white horse streaks through your tender, developing world. I was aware I was Black in the way most adolescents are aware of their gender identity. But what was knocking on the door was the knowledge of what it meant to be Black in America.

My father opened the door, and the look on his face was one of utter horror. I now know it was the look of a Black man who has had his worst American nightmare come true before his eyes. I now know the four hundred years of history and pain and blood and turmoil that was brought instantly to his consciousness. I now know what this day was to him, but on that day, I was simply curious about what was on the other side of our door. As soon as he opened it, I could feel the tension flood through the door in waves that instantly gripped him. My mom noticed too, and as I tried to get a view, she took to his side, and I saw something break in her at that moment. I don't know if she ever got it back. It was the illusion many parents of Black children fall under, that they will somehow be able to protect them from white supremacy in our land. But like my parents, they all reach a moment when that illusion is ripped away like a thin veil that, moments before, seemed a sure and steady wall of love and safety. She was wrong. As I took a better position to look out the door, I realized my parents were liars. We weren't a miracle. We were an abomination, an aberration, a mistake, and the price of that had come due. I saw my bully standing next to his father, who was dressed in blue jeans and a Confederate flag shirt. He held a shotgun so loosely, it appeared to be almost an extension of him. This was the first time I had ever seen a gun in my life. It was the first time I felt the icy-cold powerlessness of standing in front of someone brandishing a gun with hatred in their eyes. My father found his voice and said, "Can I help you?" I remember thinking how ludicrous that sounded as a response. Where was the bravado? Why didn't he take the shotgun from this guy's hands? Why wasn't he protecting us? It was the first time I knew that he couldn't protect me from whiteness. A pit in the bottom of my stomach started to spread throughout my body and turned into a terror that was moving at a fever pitch. The man replied simply, "Your nigger kids attacked my boy, and if they ever do that again, I'm going to come up here and kill you and your nigger-loving wife." The man looked at all of us, saw the fear in our eyes, and simply walked away, my bully smiling from behind a swollen forehead at me as they receded off into the evening.

Blackness is a revelation sometimes. It shows up, as it says in the book of Revelation, like a scroll being unfurled, and whole armies marching out swallow you whole. It is a trumpet that sounds and brings the tidings of war and rumors of war. It is an island you can be exiled to as a child where visions of what could be terrify you all night.

4

FREEDOM SMELLS LIKE THE BACK OF A GREYHOUND BUS

In the spring of 1991, I was thirteen years old and living my last few months at home. I had already tried to escape a few times, but now my great adventure was about to begin. I don't know if you grew up in the kind of home that I did. Where just the pattern of drunken footsteps up the stairs can freeze your heart cold. Or where the tension was so thick that you counted the pattern of drunken footfalls up the steps. Where you obsessed over the way you did the dishes or swept the floor, afraid that a slap would leave you on the floor seeing stars. Where it was like walking across an emotional landscape littered with traps and snares that at any second could grip you by your T-shirt and shatter your little world. My father had become a monster, a grotesque caricature of manhood more likely to throw me out of a window than tell me he loved me.

Have you ever been beaten to the point where not only can you not walk, but the welts feel like they are soul deep, that they are somehow imprinted with more sticking power than the image of God with which you were created? I was beginning to learn from my father—and from the great pieces of literature that I devoured—that history tends to repeat itself. Every blow felt like it was taking me closer to being just like him. Every drop of blood I lost, every red mark, every bruise, every night in fear was molding me into the weapon that would perpetuate this cycle of violence. Everything I read told me that I was being bred into a monster. In some ways, to this day, I still feel like one. I can be cold and callous to those who love me and suddenly cut off my love without warning or pattern. I create whole interior landscapes and story lines that trick me into believing I'm just not worth loving. There is an entire leviathan waiting in my subconscious, in the depths of me. Even typing these words now, I can feel the gravity well of brokenness trying to pull me down to the glass shards of yesterday, hoping to cut me wide open. If these are words that speak to you, that trace the lines of your own scars, then know I write these words for you. You aren't alone, and you can survive your own story and thrive in new ones. Sometimes when I'm reminded of what I could have been, that deformed creature peeks out of my eyes, so incredibly angry at the power of grace and healing and redemption.

You have to understand the incredible stress that my young psyche was under. You have to see me as a child being screamed at inches from my face, with spit flying in my eye. My sense of safety had been stolen from me as I looked up with eyes welling with tears and my last bits of defiance. You have to picture little caramel balled fists at my side. My bewilderment at a world that not only allowed this to happen but seemed to foster it. Escape was the only option.

I went to teachers and counselors, but in the late '80s and early '90s, mandatory reporting laws were much narrower than they are today, and I begged them not to say anything. As much as I hated my world, it was all I had, and I had seen what happens when the authorities show up. I have never seen the police show up in Black America and make a situation better. Ever.

When I was seven years old, the MOVE bombing happened. Less than ten blocks from my house, a Black liberation movement that combined anarcho-primitivism and Black nationalism had set up shop on Sixty-Second and Osage Avenue. The good people of Osage Avenue were more than fed up with them broadcasting their beliefs out of a speaker attached to the roof and didn't understand the dreadlocked children running around in the garden out back naked. MOVE had a few run-ins with the Philadelphia police, which led to stand-offs in the "bottoms" of West Philadelphia and later moving a little over a mile away to Sixty-Third and Osage Avenue. This was during the Frank Rizzo era of policing. Rizzo served as Philadelphia's police commissioner from 1968 to 1971 and as mayor of Philadelphia from 1972 to 1980. His famous policies shaped my father's childhood and cast a long shadow over mine. For example, if more than three Black teens were walking together on the same side of the street, it was considered gang activity. This gave the police carte blanche to basically harass every teen in the area, and that policy created an atmosphere of distrust among the community that was fostered by half a century of systemic racism on top of it. Rizzo's policy was to treat MOVE like an insurgent army, and this mess was inherited by Philadelphia's first Black mayor, Wilson Goode, in 1985.

I said the good people of Osage Avenue because they couldn't know what was going to happen as a result of their complaints to the city about the compound that had sprung up in the middle of their block. They made the mistake of thinking the police and the city government were on their side. It is a common mistake. You start to believe that because you own your home, work hard, and take pride in your neighborhood that the government has your best interest at heart. In my experience, this is never true if you are Black in this country. It's a lie that over the last decade has been exposed for what it is. What followed is the worst case of police brutality in American history. The police, after instigating a shootout with the armed and rightfully paranoid MOVE members, decided the next move was to drop two bombs made of Tovex, a dynamite substitute typically used for forced entry, onto the roof of the house on Osage Avenue. The two pounds of explosives (by police accounts, anyway) were dropped by helicopter. The resulting fire spread for several blocks. Eleven people died in the fire, all members of MOVE. That includes five children. MOVE refused to leave the house as it was engulfed, and the chief of police ordered the fire chief to "let the fire burn" over the radio. There is evidence that as MOVE members tried to leave, they were fired at by police and turned back to the flames for refuge. At seven years old, this was the world that my young mind digested. As I watched the smoke rise, I asked my dad what was happening. He looked at me with a seriousness only he could muster and said flatly, "Lenny, that's what happens when you call the police."

So even though those weeks in the spring of 1991 would be my last at home, I wouldn't escape this reality for years. By this I mean that the wounds, bruises, and eventual scars would be with me my whole time on the streets. I attempted at thirteen to run as far as I could. Calling for help was out of the question. My only option was a constant drumbeat in the back of my mind. Run. Run. Run. Run. Run. Run. Run.

I tried to do that too. I stole as much money as I could get my hands on and made the first trip of many to Eleventh and Filbert. The Greyhound station. I had purchased a bunch of clothes for my trip, stuffed hundreds in cash in a duffel bag, and walked into the station, afraid they wouldn't sell me a ticket. In line, I looked at the agents, searching their eyes for the most sympathetic. I hoped I wouldn't end up with the Black momma who was working the booth at the end. No Black momma would let some kid who was twelve and looked ten buy a Greyhound ticket. She had already looked me up and down with the intense curiosity that I recognized from aunties and cousins. As I approached the front of the line, a very confused gentleman walked over to her. This was exactly what I needed! As he stepped up with a host of problems, I darted for the younger-looking guy who had the air of fucking hating his job. Sometimes as a kid on the street, indifference is a miracle to be sought out. I told the guy confidently that I wanted a ticket to Daytona Beach, Florida. He barely looked up as I paid him with fresh twenties, and the long, endless ticket started to stream out of the machine. As he was folding up my ticket and placing it in the envelope, the Black momma looked up and put up a deadly finger to the man still rambling at her, that mysterious powerful finger only Black mommas have that can silence you instantly. The man understood and watched as she slowly got up and shuffled toward me. She looked at the young man, then at my ticket, and then at me and said, "Darling, you aren't running away from home, are you? He should have asked where your parents are."

My heart stopped. I was so close to freedom. To safety. At the time, I would have had all kinds of angry, frustrated ways of describing this woman. But here is the truth. Here is the stuff you are made out of, America.

Here is the golden thread that runs through you. Here is your soul, which isn't in need of redeeming as much as being dusted off and taken down from the shelf of Twitter tirades and Instagram selfies. Because when I looked her in the eyes, I saw the eyes of a loving God looking back at me. There was compassion, and love, and challenge in those eyes, and they conveyed perfect joy and a hard-earned peace that had been carved out of a world that never gives those things up easily. It was the first time I looked into the eyes of Jesus, even though I didn't know it. I looked right into the eyes of God and lied. "No, ma'am. My parents couldn't find a place to park. I am on my way to see my uncle for a few weeks."

I would do this many times over the next decade-plus to you, America. The divine would speak through strangers all over this country and ask me things like, "Are you OK? Do you need help? Where are you headed?" You are so damn incredible, America.

She looked at me with the skepticism only a Black mother could muster, smiled, and said OK and walked away. I could feel her energy washing over me—an energy I would later come to know as prayer. I snatched my ticket and searched for the anonymity of the waiting throngs. My bus came, and I was the first in line to board. I went straight to the back of the bus by the bathroom to the three seats that could double as a bed. The smell of antiseptic and urine washed over me. As the bus pulled away from the station and the loud sounds of that toilet water swooshed with each turn to the highway, it smelled like freedom. It was the smell of liberation. New life smelled like the back of a Greyhound bus.

People treat the "margins" as joyless places bereft of anything of value. In fact, talk about the "margins" is one of the most racist narratives among progressives. I, for one, have grown to loathe the term, even though I use it from time to time to code switch. It's not the "margins" to me, asshole; it's my world, it's my moral center, it's where I reside. When you talk about my whole culture being on the periphery in one breath and then panto-mime it at home, well, it's infuriating. How can we be on the margins, and yet every song you sing, every artist you like, all the fashion you steal is Black? That liberal-racist narrative doesn't capture entire cultures that are mighty fortresses of liberation. They are birthed and grown in these places that most folks use as tools of oppression— pimps selling my helplessness to you for the sake of their woke heroes' accolades and reputations.

I'm going to share with you the secret places in this country 'tis of thee. Places you walk by every day and maybe have never examined. Places that are writhing and gyrating with life and growth. With color and hues that your eyes have never seen and with sounds your ears have never heard. Worlds within this world that are rich and textured and have a depth that if you stare into them long enough, you may never truly come out. They are packed full of characters who aren't plot devices and have a history that isn't chronicled or witnessed by many. Well, except the many who are in this separate yet inter-woven world. These stories are swapped among us like sacred scripture. As Paul Simon puts it, I spent a lifetime seeking the places "Where the ragged people go / Looking for the places / Only they would know."

It was on my first Greyhound adventure when I met my friend Davester. That's his name. I would start to inhabit a world full of people who all lived by pseudonyms and stage names. We met at the Eyes of the World head shop. They had a picnic table out back where you could hear the notes of the Dead and Phish and Widespread Panic start to dot the salt-infused air. It was where I learned sex work as a survival technique. Where I started to slowly accept my sexual identity, at least quietly. It would be years before I slept with another man just for pleasure, but another street kid saw me asking for spare change and taught me how to cruise the LGBTQIA clubs and find "johns," and this was OK to me. I was making the most of my freedom and pleasure. It was revolutionary to me to be able to love any gender. For me at thirteen years old, love was sex. This first excursion into America was glorious. Coming from my home, it was goddamn utopia. The police eventually sent me home. I would start to leave every few weeks.

Eventually I saw the Jerry Garcia Band in the fall of 1993 and was utterly changed. A new friend named—wait for it—Bongo the Surf King taught me how to sell LSD and T-shirts and took me to my first Jerry show.

I was hanging with a bunch of Deadheads and traveler types at the time but had no idea what the scene was about. They were just kind to me and didn't ask me probing questions. At my first Jerry Garcia Band show—my introduction into the whole jam-band scene—I was more excited to be making money selling acid and smoking endless amounts of weed. One person asked me if I was going in, and I said I didn't know. He looked at me for a long moment and said, "Here, kid," and gave me a ticket. It was a general-admission floor ticket at the Meadowlands—at the time, I had no idea what a precious item that was. I walked in with no idea what was about to happen. I didn't know what I was expecting, but it was a wild one. I mean, the energy alone was enough to get you rocked (or grocked if you are in this scene), but I dropped a few tabs of acid just in case.

The lights went down, and a cheer erupted from the crowd. Out came three ladies who looked like they could be from any gospel choir in Philadelphia, and then Melvin Seals, a rather larger brother, came out on stage and sat down at a Hammond piano with two Leslie speakers like you would see in almost any Black church in the country. Then came this old, gray-haired, chubby white dude. He had on a black T-shirt and loose pants, and he picked up a guitar. He was old—or at least he looked weary. He flashed a smile that seemed to spark across the room, jumping from person to person. Like fireworks, but that could have also been the acid. I watched as this infectious joy from a little smirk spread from him to the rest of the crowd like a pulsing wave. Full disclosure: at this point, I was fifteen years old and had been living on the streets for two years on and off. I was pretty jaded. Who was this fat white guy with a guitar? I knew he was the Jerry Garcia I had been hearing so much about, and the tapes I heard were OK, but I mean all of this for that? I like to think that my first reaction to all of this was thoroughly West Philly. "Skeptical" is polite.

This was before I became convinced that music was the most powerful controlled substance in the world. This was before I realized the great lengths I would go to hear music that would take me to the place I was about to enter for the first time. This was before all of that. Here is what I knew: I was in a battle to survive in a world that seemed designed to destroy me, and I had found refuge, shelter from the storm, with this community of intrepid travelers. And they loved this shit, whatever it was.

I think about that night a lot. How I would OD later that night. There is much debate in this scene about whether a person can OD on LSD. More accurately, I couldn't handle what I was experiencing, and I fell out in a fit of convulsions and started to swallow my own vomit. But some folks might say that it was my very makeup being stripped and laid bare before my consciousness. That's what I couldn't handle. It wasn't the drug. I think about that night a lot. How I would take so much acid that I would stare into the screaming abyss of psychedelic experience and come back changed. I had tripped once before that night: I took thirteen hits on my thirteenth birthday because I didn't know how much you were supposed to take. Something had shifted in me, and I felt a gentleness and openness that I had never experienced in my life. That birthday is a neon fever dream full of the entire cosmos beckoning me to explore. And now that door of perception, for better or for worse, was about to be kicked open.

If they would have opened with any other song, I think my Black ass would have done the smart thing and gone back to the parking lot and just hung out there. But that night, they opened with "How Sweet It Is"— a Motown classic. And they played it in a way that it seemed the song was always begging to be played. Heavy organ riffs and a guitar that stretched each note into heaven. The backup singers became angels, and the whole world opened up to me. This would start a live music obsession in the jam-band scene that has lasted in me to this day. I didn't know that this night, this very special night, was going to start me on a journey across the contiguous states. As it turns out, I would see most of them within the year. I didn't know that I found a magical place where kids like me could dance and be free and that no one would beat me or hurt me, at least not intentionally. I didn't know that I had just stumbled into an American adventure that had been slow cooking since 1964 just for me. *If you have ever been in this scene, you know the whole thing always feels like it is just for you.* I didn't know about sexuality and the freedom of expression it·opens to you. I didn't know about traveling, alternative paths of dealing with the American thing, or the cast of thousands I was about to meet. On that night, I was like any love-struck fool, just trying to get my footing. On that night, I didn't know that the shadow side of the scene would almost kill me, or that I would have some really lonely days ahead traveling from place to place, chasing a Day-Glo circus across the country. Or that I would see this man perform dozens upon dozens of times in the two years to come. I had no idea the thing would reach a tragic end for him in 1995. All I knew is by the time the second set opened with "Shining Star"—an Earth, Wind & Fire classic—I couldn't imagine doing anything else with my time. I was young, free, and dancing like no one was looking, some-thing I do to this day.

After fifteen years on the planet, I had found safety.

I found home.

5

THE LAST GREAT AMERICAN ADVENTURE

The American adventure has been the nameless thing I have always craved. What excites me is the lure of the unknown, the unborn moment waiting to scream for its first breath and for skin-to-skin contact with the dazzling and new. What calls me out of the normal, everyday humdrum of a capitalist society are moments like this. They break the cage of white supremacy that tries to tell me that my worth is what I produce. Jack Kerouac typed the text for his book *On the Road* so fiercely, so relentlessly, as if he was trying to trap time itself on the pages, that he ran out of paper. He finished the book on toilet paper. His writing was fueled and pushed into existence by what he had seen, touched, heard, held, loved, and captured on the road. What would it take to make you stand at the edge of the Grand Canyon, look down into the ravine, and scream, howl, and wail until your throat is raw and the echoes sing back to you in tones of absolute bliss and freedom? The grand question is simply, How do you get to that place? The things that take me beyond what I know, what I think, when I run out of words and descriptions. The experiences I will recall on my deathbed are made up of moments that passed me by at sixty miles per hour, landscapes my eye only caught for a second as I moved on to the next town. The next goal. To be quickly replaced by another spot on the map.

Have you ever been so lost that you abandon your Rand McNally and your phone, which doesn't have service, and just follow the setting sun in some small town you will never see again? If you haven't, then I contend that you may not know America at all. This isn't a critique; most of us don't. Most of us haven't relied on the kindness of strangers for a meal and let our peace fall on them when we entered their home or shook the dust off our shoes of a town that has rejected us. What would it take to wake up our primal need for something unexpected, different, and hopefully a little dangerous?

I am convinced that the American adventure is a quickly dying experience. A thing that once burned brightly in our imaginations and lit whole hearts up with a passion for the unknown. If you can't tell by now, I have opinions within opinions on what ails this country, and much of it is rooted in the very core of our nation.

I believe systemic racism, patriarchy, queerphobia, colonialism, and free-market capitalism are destroying the human spirit. When I talk about the last American adventure, I'm not talking about colonialism and imperialistic visions of the "conquering" of the West. I'm talking about the recapturing of what has already been stolen by those of us who still have love in our hearts. I'm talking about being the eyes and ears of God and seeing the suffering and beauty of creation on the Divine's behalf. I'm talking about a radical revolution of values that you share at as many highway exits as possible.

As a teen, I was keenly aware of all those forces that under the intense pressure of oppression created what I would call the roots of my story and my life. Poverty and race in particular, and I knew I could never talk about being queer at home or among schoolyard friends. Queer children instinctively knew in the late '80s and '90s that to be safe, we had to be secret. No one overtly told me, "Don't tell anyone that," but my whole world screamed it. I often think about the secret worlds of children: full of hope, inspiration, and fear. How our inner universe tends to pick up transmissions from a cruel world before we are even aware of them. So while I was awake to these things, seeing them as obstructions in my personal quest for the great American adventure, I wasn't deterred. I heard the voices of Ken Kesey and Neal Cassady urging me on. I could hear the notes of Sly and the Family Stone just around the bend and all the Bobs

(Dylan, Weir, and Marley) telling me, "Go ahead, kid." You see, my inner world had been infected, infiltrated, and fed subversive thoughts since the first time I could go to a library and ask for books on my own. From Chairman Mao to Sun Tzu to Ginsberg, I trekked across the shadow side of society. I was enraptured by the *Electric Kool-Aid Acid Test* and read *Illusions: The Adventure of a Reluctant Messiah* like it was a handbook. I read Ram Dass and the Qur'an. I thought Huck Finn was a coward and a racist, but I could see that he wanted his freedom desperately. I read the *Invisible Man* and thought "The Tell-Tale Heart" wasn't as scary as Sixtieth and Vine Street back home. I saw a book titled *Steal This Book*, and I did. I devoured it like a starved ghoul. I read *The Anarchist Cookbook* at eleven. Not the sanitized version you can buy now, but the original 1971 manuscript. I read the history of the NAACP and the Willie Lynch papers when they were popular. I read about Project MKUltra when I was ten and was excited by the prospect of college experimentation on my young mind. I read all the speeches of Fredrick Douglass and held them in the same regard as Mos Def or Dead Prez.

What I'm trying to tell you is that the spirit of adventure, that spirit of something different, that siren song to tune in and drop out was something that was always encoded into my very makeup. Every atom in my body was interested in that thing that has inspired artists, birthed innovations, caused whole subcultures to rise up, and fed leaders into the great maw of the American empire.

I'm trying to share with you the ingredients of the recipe that led me as a young kid to try the last American adventure: hitchhiking.

Even now it seems so long ago and a strange time in our history when people would head to the interstate, walk down an exit, and stick their thumb out. I mean, I even made signs that read, "San Francisco or Bust." How absurd would that be today? While writing this book, I moved across the country. I drove all the way from Brooklyn, New York, to Vancouver, Washington, and I didn't see one hitchhiker. I can't tell you how heartbroken I was. I mentioned to my wife that I was going to pick up any hitchhiker I saw, and the panic in her voice was palpable. That's when I knew I would be writing this chapter to celebrate this forgotten piece of American folklore.

I don't remember the first car that picked me up. I mean, you would think I would remember the fear or the car or the driver, but nope. None of it. By the time I started hitching regularly, I was fifteen and had already spent two years "on the road," as I called it. The great highway. For me, that meant anywhere other than where I had been and having no idea what would become of me. That feeling of not knowing what would happen next, what the night would look like, who would pick me up, what world they were dragging around the country with them, it was intoxicating. Each ride was like a little glimpse into the fabric of this country. Across cultural barriers and socio-economic borders. I leaped into the middle of sales trips or tagged along on evangelism trips. I hopped in vans on the way to the same festival I was going to or rode with people running from the crushing weight of broken lives left behind. Kindred souls who were sure that just beyond the next state border, a better day waited to ambush them with something holy. Something that was full of new life and new creation. Something that would change the trajectory their life was on. Something that would alter their course.

It is the foolish hope of America. It is undefinable, unquenchable, and when it has ahold of you, it seizes your dreams and life and hardly ever lets go. The way it shows up in your life shifts through the years, but the truth is, it never really goes anywhere. I still get that feeling when I'm in a car driving sometimes. *Road hypnosis* is another term for it, when good music is playing and the scattered communities of Middle America are flying by at seventy-five miles per hour. As you speed past roadside attractions, diners, and the gossamer things and events strung together that create a life and a home. Hitchhiking in the '90s was all those things but hyperaccelerated into bite-sized bits of mystery.

I don't remember that first ride, but I remember other parts of the first day vividly. I remember a creaking Ford truck that cut over three lanes to pick me up and skidded to a stop about a hundred yards away. I took off running at full speed to reach it. It's as if those one hundred yards contain the entire world; all space and time are at your fingertips. It's as if you could split open the universe in that moment, and all things are yours to access. In those one hundred yards, the dice of fate are rolling, and you are just hoping for one more seven or eleven or at least to match the number from the last ride. In those one hundred yards, you are free.

I looked in the window, smiled, and got the question that would define my life for the next decade-plus: "Where you headed?" This time I answered, "South." But as time went on, it would be any of the cardinal directions. I learned that it's easier to answer west or east than nowhere at all. That's not to say I didn't have a vague idea of where I was headed—typically to catch up with the Grateful Dead tour, or to a festival, or to a town that I was told was some sort of subculture utopia where the herb was plentiful and the police scarce. But a growing sense was planted in my soul those first few rides that my home was this now: the side of the road of the passenger seat of a car playing navigator for a stranger turned friend turned stranger again.

When I was first introduced to the concept of sexuality being fluid, it was much later in life. But it fit into my paradigm because I was used to being a lover and companion to whoever loved me back for most of my formative years. It never seemed strange; it was natural. Powerful. Life giving. And it didn't always involve sex.

I could say my home most of the time while hitchhiking around this country was love. Companion was my code. Fidelity meant simply adhering to this code as freely as possible. Whatever didn't feel like freedom, you walked away from. This was a sacred duty, and you would find others who honored this sacred place with you. Like two travelers huddling around a fire for warmth, the fire being mystery and the warmth being each other. Sometimes, if you were really lucky, you would meet others who wanted to see that fire spread and become a funeral pyre for the whole damn system. To watch the sparks become little flames that would spread over the kindling of the capitalist dystopia that was slowing lurching toward its death. As the flames licked at the edges of society, you would find those willing to cheer it on, or throw a concert at its edge, or form a community right in its damned center. Those communities would be home for a while as you sought the next place that only the ragged people go. Skipping like a rock across the surface of what most people called the everyday, never sinking below the surface and defying the gravity of the mundane. It would be years before the mundane attracted me, and at the time, I would have denied it ever could. I just needed the proper amount of force and the right angle, and I could go on like this forever.

This was before the rough patches. Before drugs and alcohol owned my everything. Before the things most people picture happening to a thirteen-year-old kid on the road by themselves. Before the sexual assaults. Before the almost lynching in Georgia. Before the scary days in the shadow places where the sun couldn't seem to pierce. Before I found myself wandering a major city alone during the holidays starving for connection. Before the days of desperation when hunger was a constant companion and dumpster diving felt like my only option. Before the first time the existential loneliness of the American nightmare got ahold of me. Before the prison-industrial complex started to sink its claws in me. Before the bruises my father left resurfaced until I was a walking wound. Before I became everything that I swore to a God I wasn't sure was even there I would never become. Before nine-year-old Lenny couldn't look me in the eyes anymore.

On this day, it was all freedom. On this day, it was the lure that only green highway signs could invoke in me. On this day, it was the last great American adventure. It was kind people who picked me up and told me their stories. They would drive me a hundred miles out of their way so I would have a better chance of getting a ride. They would stuff a hundred-dollar bill in my hand and politely ask me if I wanted to pray. They would invite me into their homes and offer shelter from the storm. You see, it is on this day, America, when I saw what you were made of, and it was complex, messy, diverse, and so incredibly fucking hopeful. You who had penned me up in poverty, who had passively participated in my destruction, who had turned a blind eye to my community—you met me with hope in my eye and inspiration wrapped around my head like a halo, and you stared right back at me with the same look in your own eyes. You saw me on a highway exit and stopped. You found me with broken wings and taught me to fly. You told me about your lives, lovers, families, and friends. You shared your gifts and your dreams and your God. You too were bewildered by the brokenness of the world and were trying to avoid the jagged edges of this life. You too had scars and wounds that were still healing. America, I have seen you—I mean, really seen you—from the endless corn-fields to the Rockies. To your Black communities nestled in cities with so much of that fucking raw divine energy that makes Blackness so glorious. I have jumped in the Atlantic right before the beginning of a ride and got out of that same ride in the same week and jumped in the Pacific. I have chased the horizon with you and crossed time zones off like a checklist at the local grocery store. I have seen you worship in the middle of a field and in cathedrals. I have watched you wake up and give it another go. I have seen you rise to the occasion and hide from the times.

America, I have touched you. I have run my hands along your sides and felt the curves of your struggles and the dip in your joy. I have held you so close that our heart-beats have become one. I have been pressed so close to you, I can't tell where you begin and I end anymore. I have been punched in the gut by you and felt butterflies in my stomach after looking you in the eyes. I have felt your soft lips slowly make their way down my chest with a devilish grin on your face. I have sat in tattoo parlors as you have embedded your scenery up and down my arms, leaving me a work of rather strange art. I have had you choke the life out of me and woke up three days later ready to give it another chance. I have washed your worn feet from a walk that never seems to end, and you have washed mine. I have played with your hair and been delighted in the colors and textures of it.

America, laying aside our leaders and our institutions, our squabbles and our very real systems of oppression just for a second, you amaze me. I am in awe of you.

And that is because sometime in the '90s, you pulled over your Ford truck, creaked to a halting stop, and picked me up, and the adventure began. And for that reason, I'll always love you.

6

MY QUEER AF '90S, OR WHY I WOULD RATHER FUCK SLATER

I am queer, but we wouldn't have called it that in the '90s. At that time, we found ourselves living in a strange sort of in-between space. The world was ready for more acceptance, but that same world would soon tie Matthew Shepard to a fence and leave his near-lifeless, tortured body there. When Matthew died, so did some of our hopes of ever being accepted. The whole nation was riveted by this story in 1998 and how the murderers' only defense was simply that Matthew had flirted with them. I mean, think about that for a second. Just twenty-three years before I sat down to write this book, a viable defense in a court of law for the execution of a queer person in this country was white heteronormative discomfort with a young gay man's very sexuality. I couldn't come out to that world.

The configurations, frameworks, and gatherings that I found love in were illicit and underground. I sought solace in the same ragged edges of society where others like me did. We were the forgotten generation, and in many ways, we were OK with it. Most kids I met on the streets of America were queer or queer adjacent. We were the first to take the term *queer* back from being an epithet and turn it into an identity. A revolutionary renaming or rebirth.

Our very lives were dripped, submerged, soaked in this new water of life. The first time I kissed someone of the same gender with a group of friends, it felt like I could finally breathe. We all kissed each other as we lay there and allowed ourselves to just be. My father would often call me *faggot*, *homo*, or other names as he beat me. Even though he'd seen that I was attracted to women, he must have sensed that I was also attracted to anyone. And that, I think, was the thing in the '90s that was the clearest to me. We were no longer relegated to cultural references or tucked away into a corner of your city, but here we all were looking up at you as children calling you Mom and Dad. That was the betrayal America felt. That its children were turning against them the same way they had just a generation prior, and we made their rebellion seem old, sterile, fruitless, and broken. Theirs was rendered inert by their revulsion to what we had become. No one *wants* to become the establishment, and as I get older, it is a constant battle to not become the very thing

I hate. Age and time are merciless in their attacks upon what once made us bold enough to stand on the very bleeding edge. Slowly, they drag us to obscurity and relegate us to the secret place where hope goes to retire. I say this because I can't become bitter, and I refuse to let the hatred of others change or warp me. Defiance in the face of crushing societal adversity may not be a personality, but it certainly is a defining characteristic of mine. The most dangerous thing about defiance is that it can start to cut you to ribbons. If you aren't superdiligent, the very thing that brought you to a place of resistance, which I believe is love, can be lost. That, I think, is evil's ultimate victory, when you become so broken by the fight, you no longer remember why you entered the fray in the first place. I mean, really remember. In the deep, untouched places of your spirit—rooted in experiences like the first time you kissed a lover, stood in the middle of a crowd at a protest and felt hope, saw someone being bullied or receiving hatred and intervened, made art in the middle of tragedy, grabbed a book you weren't supposed to.

I remember the first time I went to the "Gayberhood" in Philadelphia. (I didn't make the name up, and it's a proud title for most folks in that community.) I was eleven or twelve, and I went into a queer bookstore. It was a revelation. Sandwiched between rainbow flags, decor, and the odd sex toy were books about every question I had ever had about the way I seem to be wired differently than everyone else. I stole several books, hid them, read them, then got rid of them. That's what it was like to be queer in the '90s. You felt you were undercover all the time, and whatever information you received from your people you destroyed like orders the enemy must not find. It felt subversive with a sense of downright revolutionary defiance in the face of forces out to destroy you. I'm not sure I have that sense today, not that things have changed that much for the better; it just felt different back then. Maybe it was the way I struggled to survive as a teen on my own, or maybe it was just my youthful perspective, or maybe it was just a different age. And my radicalization and liberation took place in more than just secret nights with lovers; they played out on the streets of America for all to see. Like a macabre play, I knew the tragic ending of every kid that was predestined, predetermined, and had an awful gravity that none would escape.

When you're homeless in this country, it's easy to have the sense that all the world is passing you by on its way to the important work of society but is pausing to gawk for a second. To take in the absurdity of the situation. To watch you as you rise from the ashes of the places they thought they had long burned down with indifference and hatred. This also gives you a sense that everyone knows. You are not sure what everyone knows, *but they know*. They know that you are on something or don't have anywhere to be, or they can see your scarred spirit and the wounds festering in your soul. They know that your life is harder than theirs, that there is probably no escape for you and things will eventually go very poorly for you. They know that you are their brothers and sisters back home who may not fit into that particular binary. They know you are their classmates and coworkers; they know you are who they themselves could be given the wrong turn in life or different level of privilege. Some of them know you are their sibling in the divine. But the sense that everyone knows and sees is a huge part of being homeless. The sense that you live in a glass bowl for all the world to judge, measure, and find wanting is something that is impossible to escape when on the streets.

And yet there is so much that people don't see. I want to tell you about the incredible worlds within worlds I discovered in this country. The secret place where homeless teens hid in the '90s. It wasn't a place as in a specific location—it was on Haight Street in San Francisco, in the lofty space between Golden Gate Park, the Castro District, and the Fillmore District. It was on Thirteenth Street in Boulder, Colorado, or in Eugene, Oregon. Both, at the time, had an Antica Roma coffee shop at the end of the block and a motley cast of teens willing to sell you a bag or herb or busk a song or just chat you up for a smoke. It was in Broad Ripple in Indianapolis, Indiana, and nestled in Westport in Kansas City. It was a hazy, smoke-filled room in Eureka, California, on someone's land you were brought to blindfolded because they were growing acres of herb. It was in Oakland and Telegraph in Berkley at People's Park. It was everywhere, wherever "those" people gathered. In my hometown, Philadelphia, that place was South Street. These bastions of free thought and bad decisions where the regular order of what everyday life was suspended for just a few moments every night and you could just be. I mean really just be. You could find this place at festivals, on jam-band tours, at national rainbow gatherings, or even in the early days of Burning Man—all the weird scenes that this country just seemed to be packed with. The lifeblood of these places was queer folks. As I said earlier, most of the teens I knew on the streets were either queer or queer adjacent. I have started to wonder what my contribution to queer history and more specifically Black queer history is. The things I know, the things that are sewn into the tapestry of my own queer story, are these days on the road. I have had younger queer folks tell me that there was a language for what we were experiencing at the time. There was community. There was what I see today as a thriving and gorgeous way of life. But I have to tell you, we didn't have access to it. I didn't have access to it.

The Castro District doesn't look too inviting from the sidewalk when quarters are tossed at you by passersby. Were the folks there more understanding and loving? One hundred percent. But did it seem like a world you had access to when you were wondering where you will sleep, if that cop is going to stop and hassle you, if that group will give you the change you are short on for food, and if the boy in the group is cute? No. It seems an impossible dream—your scene, your safe place, is out of reach. In the '90s, and today, a person first needs to obtain a certain amount of economic security and privilege before they can express who they really are. The ability to take time to reflect and grow and live into the fullness of who you are is something that only those firmly in the middle class or above in the economic strata that is America can do easily. Spiritual and mental growth need room to thrive, and when your day is crowded with basic survival or, like me at times, drug addiction caused by trauma and genetic predisposition, well, you don't just get a lot of "me time" or self-care.

So while places existed where I could have learned about queer history or queer theology or culture as a teen, I simply didn't have a ton of ways to access them. I just got to witness them. Watch them play out before I folded myself back into the shadow world I existed in that seemed to mirror everyone else's but never let me quite touch it. In that mirror, I could gaze deeply into my own experience and see it reflected in the lives of people who either got a better break or just got lucky.

That's a thing people don't ever think about enough, just how arbitrary it all is in the United States. How one bad week can change the entire trajectory of generations of your family. Capitalism is an unrelenting and unforgiving host, and we all seem to be living in its home. I think you can't fully appreciate this until you are seated right out on the edge of the opulence that is everyday American life. Until the first time someone throws away Styrofoam leftovers in front of you, ignores you, and walks on as you wait for them to turn the corner to grab those leftovers out of the trash can. Then as you sit to have your meal, sharing it with the huddled masses of friends who are out there with you, only then do you see this country. Some of those gathered were on the lookout for white vans that would pull up and snatch them to reparative therapy camps. Predatory "deprogramming" groups that parents would hire to hunt us like big game in the new home we were creating and who struck in broad daylight to take some of us to places where they prayed away the gay. Some of us were on the lookout for johns and would offer our bodies to situations where consent was often questionable due to power dynamics and age, which I had to hide like a secret identity. I can tell you that there were times when sex work felt empowering and wonderful and other times where it felt like just a way to survive. Like any human experience, it runs the gamut, and it doesn't fit into any mold. Certainly, my experience isn't the normative one, and it doesn't compare with what folks experience nowadays with the advent of the internet age. I'm supposed to feed the neoliberal narrative here about how sad those times were for me and how degrading. I refuse. Some of the best sex I had and friends I made at the time were a result of sex work, and there were times when I loved it. There were times when it was all I wanted to do. There were times when I was in unsafe situations, but by definition, at that time, my entire life was an unsafe situation. I was a queer Black teen on the streets of America with no real home to return to and certainly had no parents sending the proverbial bloodhounds out to find me. I had been sent home by well-meaning municipalities several times during my life on the streets. Sent back to my abuser, who now feared me because of the boldness I came home with. I had faced the world and had come back forged as something else. Something different. My father's small and broken world held no sway over me. In fact, there was this silent assent between us as a family. I was no longer an indoor cat and had to be let outside to scratch, wail, scream, and wander. To be honest, it was easier for my parents to go about their addiction without me around. One less mouth to feed and no one who challenged them. My brother had been captured by the streets of West Philadelphia, whose death toll and survivability rate were much tougher than the game I was playing. I had become something of a local legend in my neighborhood; when I would be sent back, the neighbors watched with side-eyes and whispers. I mean, I came home dreaded, pierced, and tatted in a time when very few Black folks in my area were into that sort of thing. People who I grew up with would ask me where I had been, and I would say something like Los Angeles or Chicago. Worlds they had read about but never seen. They would wait for the day I would angrily walk away from my house with a JanSport packed full of the trinkets of my life and head toward the El. I would hop on a Greyhound and be gone again. Years at a time.

I would run again to these worlds that were created out of strings of love and chords that hinted at melodies of peace and understanding. Whole compositions of unspoken but deeply understood invitations to be who you truly are. To take off the mask that we all had to wear wherever we were running from and to see each other's secret faces that only came out at times when the world seemed ready to change. Ready to become the place of grace and hope that we were building and rebuilding all over the country. This is the ethereal cathedral where I experienced Jesus. The first time I saw the greatest commandment lived out—that we should love our neighbors as ourselves—I was in Hemlock Alley in San Francisco waiting for the needle exchange with a friend who had to get his morning medicine so he wouldn't be sick. I was fifteen years old, and it had been a cold, rainy, and tough winter for me. I looked like roadkill and hadn't had a shower in a while. Then Jesus walked up. Jesus was a Black transwoman who asked me if I was OK: what was I doing, where was I staying? The kindness in that moment. The waves of love emanating from her. She heard my lies with the practiced ear of someone who was used to kids like me on the streets lying for their own protection. She smiled, and it struck me how goddamn beautiful she was and how impressed and flattered I was that she was stopping to talk to me on the sidewalk in her fashionable heels and miniskirt. To this day, she remains one of the most beautiful women I have ever seen. I think of her there, the morning light behind her like a halo. She took me by the hand like we were a couple and got me a hotel room. She had me strip out of my clothes and took them to the washroom down the hallway. She went out for a few hours and came back with money, some new clothes, and some food. She held me that night, never once crossing any boundaries that my scattered emotional state clearly called for. I woke up, and she was gone like an angelic visitation. My clothes folded neatly at the end of the bed. Jesus folded my clothes and held me all night long. I hadn't been held by someone in so long, and her touch was healing.

This kind of thing only happened to me in queer community. Or in the weird subcultures queer community ran through like a falling star across the night sky. So I was queer in the '90s, but we wouldn't have called it that. Not to you, America. You were dangerous, the palm that held us sometimes harshly and sometimes gently.

7

SAINT NOBODY

The Faces You Never Remember

I want to tell you a story about the fickle way that life and death can be decided. It takes a cast of thousands for someone like me to be alive. The mural that is my life is full of the rich colors and brushstrokes painted into thousands of faces I can't remember. It's funny the things that linger after the slow erosion of one's memories with the relentless passage of time. What reflecting back on one's life through the lens of grace can reveal. The moments that if you would have known what they were, how they would end, you would have held on to them. You would have grabbed them in a bear hug and let the smell linger on. You would have kissed their feet and greeted them as an old friend from a life forgotten, or perhaps a life as it could be. You would have, like the apostle Peter after witnessing the transfiguration, wanted to build a shrine around them. I have often heard that story as an example of what not to do when you encounter the divine, but I'm not sure. I think we should enshrine moments like this, when the supernatural or destiny itself seems to poke through the veil just enough to remind us how loved we are. I think we should build temples of art and music and laughter and love around them. Mostly because it's so damn easy and devastating when you realize one passed you by.

I have spent much of my life seeking God. The Divine. The Universe. Even a Goddess or two. Not chasing enlightenment but certainly not avoiding it. I'm not talking about the false reverence of ideology and dogma or even theology. No, the reverence that comes from a close encounter with God. You know what I'm talking about; it's fucking biological the way you react. It's the feeling in your gut that you are somewhere you aren't supposed to be witnessing something you aren't supposed to. Yet you are exactly where you are supposed to be. It's why the first thing angels say is, "Do not be afraid!" It's terrifying.

I'm talking about when the universe for a split second drops its everyday facade and sneaks a peek at you from behind its mask of feigned indifference. I have chased those moments my whole life. I have found them on mountainsides, on sidewalks, in concerts, and occasionally in churches. I have spent a lifetime cultivating an ear for when moments like this may happen.

I'm not some spiritual master. Even now, it's rare for me to recognize, in the moment, that God is also present.

I often suspect that maybe God is up to something, that something magical is happening that I rarely know. Looking back over my life, I can see now that I was hunting these moments of perfect safety and synchronicity in the nearness of God, but at the time, I wouldn't have had a language for that. I would have said in my teens that I was looking for a place that "felt" right. I would have said something vague about vibrations or energy pieced together by scraps of scared traditions I had picked up on the way. When you spend a decade traveling around with those moments as your North Star, a couple of things happen. The first is you meet the best this land has to offer. Fellow believers in the secret story of America. The one told in the back of barrooms and the lines of festivals. On street corners and sometimes in shooting galleries. A history written in graffiti in bathrooms across the country. I mean, really the good stuff. I was born starving for the good, and this country can be a feast of good if we open ourselves up to it. You encounter the dispatches from the heart of America. People who are stunning in their beauty and incredibly powerful in their depth. Folks who are part of your story for as long as a ride or are just traveling in the same direction.

You are golden, beloved. I have met thousands upon thousands of y'all, and I have to tell you, for the most part, you are so easy to love. I have never met anyone not worth loving, and I have never failed to see the sacred in you. This is one of those stories.

It's about a kid named Saint Nobody. I can't remember his name because of the trauma of this story, and even as I type, I feel my body beginning to react—the numbness setting in. It's like trying to type underwater. I don't remember if he approached me or I him in that small town in North Carolina. It was the summer of 1993, and I was hitchhiking down 95 to get to Florida because I was a dumb kid from the Northeast and that sounded like a place to go. I remember the weather coming out of Asheville just being the kind of picture-perfect scene that only the Southeast in the mountains can give you. It felt like being in the clouds while making out with the sun. For the life of me, I don't remember how we met or his name.

I do remember his eyes—blue—and his brown hair. The stuff we cling to in memories.

This is a story of how I was almost lynched in Georgia.

I can't remember if I convinced him to come along or if he just had nothing else better going on. I do know that after several days on the road, I wasn't sure if I genuinely trusted him or just had a crush. I would keep my crushes hidden and stuffed deep down at the time, and that could have been it, but I do know I really liked him. We told our stories in the way runaways and the ragged often do, general outlines of a story often earmarked by abuse, or rejection, or sometimes just genuine curiosity for the world. I remember thinking this kid was just out here for adventure. I, on the other hand, was running and that felt incredibly different.

One night, we walked out in a Georgia field. The sky felt so close, you could pluck the stars out of the heavens and put them in your bag to always carry with you. The hush of the night when shepherds are known to hear trumpets and when the moon dances slowly across the night sky in an ancient, silent routine that moves the very waters of the earth. It was on a night like that that we lay in the grass, looking up at our slice of the celestial. In the morning, the hush of the dawn was met with dew that reflected rainbows all over each blade, and I remember distinctly waking up eye level with the dew and catching the glint of the sun on several drops. Of breathing the moment in deeply.

Saint Nobody got up and stretched and suggested we hit the road to catch a rush-hour ride. We had a fairly successful day and got a few rides, and one had even given us about one hundred bucks to get something to eat. I remember we walked into a Waffle House after 11 p.m. that night. We knew we were stuck wherever we were until at least the morning. We stopped to grab a bite, and I was hopeful that maybe we could talk ourselves into some floor space in someone's home or even find our next ride. We must have spent a few hours just talking to waitresses, chatting with other booths, telling our story in that excited way only the truly hopeful and innocent can.

Eventually a group of guys a booth over offered to drop us down the road fifty miles. I had made connections like this one hundred times on this trip alone. Are moments themselves innocent? Can they be crystallized in childlike wonder and encased in the deep rosy quartz of genuine affection for the world and the people in it? If they could, this would be that quintessential moment for me. If you could walk up to that parking lot now and peek through the window over the yellow booths and lino-leum floors. To the counter and see me sitting there with my bag and Saint Nobody. Listen to us chatter on about all the adventure, romance, and destiny that lie just around the next bend of the highway. Smell the wafting overcooked coffeepot and bacon smoke and just let it hit you for a second, then maybe you can understand the absurdity of the naivete and innocence of it all.

You see, we got in that car. I sat in the passenger seat, and Saint Nobody was squashed in between two of them in the back. The driver smiled at me pleasantly as he started the car and began chatting with his buddies in the back about the song playing. Some top-forty classic rock tune that, as a hitchhiker, you learn to recognize because every fifty miles, you get to hear the same playlist over and over again. He mentioned he wasn't taking 95 but would drop us by the exit, and I remember looking back in the rearview mirror, but Saint Nobody didn't notice. The guys in the back had broken out some gin and were encouraging him to drink. It was the look of the driver as he watched through the rearview the scene playing out behind us that first told me we were in danger as we slipped into the night.

Saint Nobody was oblivious, and I was paralyzed with fear. The driver looked at his friends and said, "Hey, give this guy some." He pointed at me. They handed the jug of gin up to me, and I looked at it on my lap as I started to see the trap unfolding before us. Saint Nobody was already slurring his words when he joined the cheers for me to take a shot. I took a small one to quiet them down, but the driver looked at me and said, "Come on, man, don't be a pussy. Look at your friend." By this time, Saint Nobody was drinking from another bottle—Jack Daniel's, by the look of it. He smiled at me and said, "It's cool, man."

I knew the next moves I made would be the difference between life and death. The tension from my suspicion had started to snake toward the back of the car as we pulled off to a state forest byway. I looked at the gin as all three sets of eyes watched me. I tried to decide how to take a hefty enough swig of this crap to satisfy the driver but small enough that I could keep my wits about me for my next move. I was screaming all this with my eyes at Saint Nobody as I took a huge gulp and wiped the white-hot burn from my chin. Everyone laughed, and the mood settled down as the driver visibly relaxed for a second. I wasn't much of a drinker at this point in my life, and I was visibly swooning to the laughter of the two in the back. Saint Nobody joined in, not even knowing this is the dance of a predator playing with its prey. Just then I looked out the window and noticed we were in the pitch black of the state forest and we had slowed down.

Have you ever watched someone contemplate violence against you? Watched murder dance in their eyes as they wonder what they will do to you? I watched that unspoken primal language pass between those who I now knew were our captors. Saint Nobody bummed a smoke off our new "friends." I wasn't surprised when the gun came out, but I was hypnotized by the silver glint of the chamber where six bullets or six lives are placed one by one to meet their end. The barrel in the moonlight as the guy right behind me held it tight in his meaty hands covered in hair and hatred. He asked, "You boys ever shoot a gun?"

The words hung in the center of the car with the smoke from Saint Nobody's cigarette. It was at that moment that he finally realized the danger we were in. It was at that moment, as we looked at each other in the rearview mirror, that his eyes sent me the story of everything he ever was or ever would be. It was in that moment that I became the bearer of this part of his story.

I spoke up and said, "I have—"

The guy cut me off by bashing the back of my head with the pistol grip. As I saw stars and the corners of my eyes threatened me with the looming darkness that only a blow like that can bring, I heard him say, "Shut up, nigger. I'm talking to the white boy back here. We know you niggers know guns."

He looked at Saint Nobody and asked, "Why you traveling with this nigger anyway? You some faggot?" I started to feel consciousness fade, and I grabbed the door desperately to hold on—that's when I knew what I had to do. I unlocked the door—I could already see the rocks and dust and trail kicking up behind us in the satanic red of the brake lights in the rearview mirror. Tears welled up as I looked Saint Nobody in the eyes and tried to tell him everything. That I'm sorry for my cowardice, that I'm sorry I'm not strong enough to save him, that I'm sorry he followed me, that I don't want to die like this.

I grabbed the handle and leaped. I hit the ground hard—we were going at least thirty miles per hour—and rolled to a skidding stop in a pile of gravel. I remember this vividly because I landed on my stomach and elbows, and my legs swung around to face the car. I saw it screech to a stop about fifteen yards down the road. I could see now the struggle begin in the back of the car as Saint Nobody tried to escape. I looked to the tree line, scrambled to my feet, and darted for it at full speed. I saw the driver get out and the glint of a gun over my shoulder, and that's the last time I looked back. The boom of the gun sent me running down a steep hill at full speed. I heard the sounds of someone following me into the woods. What happened next probably saved my life.

As I turned, I hit a tree at full speed—so hard, I knocked myself out and slid into a gully between two

trees. I woke up the next day covered in puke and stag-
gered to the road. Other than the swerve marks, I saw
no clue what happened to that kid with the brown hair
and blue eyes I call Saint Nobody. His name erased from
my memory by trauma and his face faded by the passage
of time.

I eventually found a state forest camp area and
cleaned myself up in the restroom. The numb horror of
that morning sticks with me. But you know what I remember more than anything? The walk with Saint Nobody
by the side of the highway that magical night in the field
where the cosmos opened up for us. I remember his easy
smile and the kind way he talked to me. No one in my life
at fifteen years old was kind to me. I remember him because
he was with me when the world seemed full of endless
possibilities and before I realized the horror of some of
those possibilities. He was my friend before I understood
white supremacy as a system or before I could verbalize
it. He is my patron saint. I remember him because he was
with me when you showed me your most ugly disguise,
America. And he was grace. He was grace to a little boy
lost on his own in America with no friends to call his own.
He is a saint in the great cloud of witnesses no matter what
happened that night. I often think of him and the joy
of him, just the joy of being around him. I thought
that America dressed up as those monsters whose car
we got in, but it was actually him. Saint Nobody the
tender, whose ministry is crafted from the forgotten.

O Saint Nobody, *patron saint of hitchhikers, roadside attractions, and Waffle Houses,*
You who smell of hope, promise, burned coffee, and bacon,
Sweet guardian of futures untold and fates unknown,
May you grant me this one boon, grant me the power and will,
The holy anger and wisdom to burn white supremacy to the fucking ground with my dying breath.
Amen.

8

SIXTEEN IN SOLITARY

It would be hard to tell my story as a Black man in America and not talk about the prison-industrial complex. One cannot wade through the four-hundred-year flood that is oppression in this country and not be affected by this new enslavement of people of color. Nor can you ever underestimate the influence this predatory system has over what Blackness is allowed to mean in America, *what is permissible Blackness.* Even if you haven't encountered the so-called justice system like I have, if you are Black in this country, the policing of your body and personhood has changed the entire trajectory of your life. The constant public negotiation of what it means to be Black in society. The constant surveillance of your every move, being in a state of constant vigilance that becomes a part of your daily walk. The stress. Just moving through the day or walking into a room. The constant mental gymnastics: Are they looking at me because they are nice? Is that why they are smiling? Is it because I have invaded this white space with my presence? Are they uncomfortable? Am I? Is it me?

These negotiations start to whittle away at your soul and leave you a hollowed-out husk that was once brimming with life and resistance. Teeming with revolution. Instead, you are worn down until there is nothing left. White supremacy is relentless, and I expect to one day meet one of a thousand ends reserved for uppity niggers who have the nerve to thrive despite all the odds. Whether death by law enforcement or death by surviving in a country not designed for me to survive in, death is the only option. Whether it is the death of all hope and my spirit or my body crushed under a state trooper's boot. The only door that is opened for me with surprising regularity by America is the one that returns me to dust. This brutal reality explains my fascination with resurrection. And I know I have waxed poetically about what this country is and could be up to this point. But to understand my America, I have to take you to some dark places. One of those places is administrative segregation, or AdSeg. Or the hole. I prefer the term the hole. Solitary confinement.

I was subjected to this human torture throughout my teens and adulthood. I wouldn't have described it to you this way at the time, and maybe before COVID-19 and intentional, compassionate social distancing, most people wouldn't be able to empathize with what I'm trying to describe to you. But it was torture. There is a reason the most punitive thing you can do to a human being around the world short of killing them is cutting them off from community. I, like many others in the criminal justice system, experienced this often. Many formerly incarcerated folks, when asked about being put in isolation, will laugh it off. "It's no big deal," they will say. I did the same thing. Whether it is from the special brew of toxic masculinity that only prison can create or it's a trauma response, I don't know, but I would brush off an experience that was known for breaking people's spirits in half. It's very likely if you go to jail, you will end up in isolation. In my case, I ended up in solitary just for being me.

You see, fresh-faced smart-asses who aren't into real crime don't do well in jail. I'm just going to be honest: I wasn't a tough guy or a hardened criminal. My first encounters with what this country calls law enforcement started innocently enough. *Most abusive relationships do.* If you're a cop and you see a fifteen-year-old kid hitchhiking down the freeway, you stop. Anybody paying attention would see me passing through and think to themselves, *There is a story here.* I played a game of cat and mouse in those early years, learning to not stand out in a crowd so no one realized I was running around the country unattended or wasn't being reared by anyone but the subcultures of the time. Things like buying a new outfit every few days since I had nowhere to wash my clothes regularly. Hanging out with kids my age and just blending in as a kid who just moved into the area. I had started to cultivate survival techniques that helped me avoid being hassled as I moved through this country. Honestly, it's not hard to pick up right now, pack a bag, and leave your life. You would be surprised how quickly you would adapt and the world would provide. If you are a teenager in this country, no one is really paying attention to you anyway. It's easy to slip from one community to another. In fact, the farther from your own social context, the better. No one likes where they are from or the people in their town, but they sure love showing folks around. It's one of the great contradictions of traveling; you get to discover incredible beauty through the eyes of someone who can't see it anymore. Some of the most enduring friendships of my life sprang from connections like this. Take my friend Jim. We met in the summer of 1994 in the Grand Teton National Park in Wyoming. We were both there for an event called the National Rainbow Gathering. Don't get excited; it's not as cool as it sounds. I want to be fair to the group of Americans in the '90s who called themselves the "Rainbow Family." It is or was a patchwork network of subculture folks who leaned more toward the crunchy side of the scene, but not always. Some were travelers like me who had no roots. Some were very rooted, with jobs in the straight world, but owned farms, collectives, or communes or just spent a few months out of the year on the road with me. Some were radicals left over from the '60s, '70s, and '80s and had just decided they wanted no part of the American thing, as it was known. There was a "phonebook" published once a year of everyone who belonged to the Rainbow Family and was willing to list their landline and address. It was a network composed of mutual trust, collective sharing, some real earnest belief in moving the world toward a better future, and, of course, a few bad actors, like every group. But that phonebook was almost always a guaranteed place to stay in every state in the union. For me, other than the Grateful Dead tour in the '90s, it was one of the only scenes I could make connections all over the country. Friendships that could endure the lifestyle many of us had chosen.

What does any of this have to do with prison? Relax, dear reader, you will get your poverty porn of me melting in a cell all by myself, but let me paint the entire scene for you first. It's important that you see the disparate and innocent threads that were eventually woven together to become a noose around my neck. It will help you develop the ability to notice it in your own community and life.

Jim and I met at the 1994 national gathering of this community of folks. Picture in your mind's eye at least several thousand hippies, yoga instructors, artists, witches, runaways, travelers, bikers, stoner kids, dharma bums, punk rock train hoppers, fairies and nymphs, musicians, magic school buses, Dead Heads and Phish kids, plain ol' weirdos, pranksters, writers looking for "life experience," performers from several underground circuses, and everything else the underground could spit out. Picture all those folks in a national forest site, setting up a temporary infrastructure with its own economy and an open-air market. This is the scene I landed in—or, more accurately, when my ride dropped me off a few miles from the site, I hiked the rest of the way to. I ran into Jim on the wrong school bus, where I ended up being fed way too many peyote buttons via a potent tea by an unhinged white hippie woman who claimed to have supernatural powers. I thought it was the silver bus I came in on, but it clearly wasn't. She gave me a second cup to give a friend. Jim, a complete stranger, was standing around. I started talking to him, and I could already feel my sense of reality slowly collapsing in on itself. I started to panic. Jim agreed to drink the second cup with me so I wouldn't melt alone. This is the danger of Indigenous and native culture in the hands of white people. At the time, I was sixteen and not very smart. Now I see how dangerous the situation was and how problematic it was for me to assume I had any right to partake in peyote—which has been used in sacred rituals and medicinally by Indigenous Americans for centuries. But the truth is, I just didn't know better. What Jim did that day was the psychedelic equivalent of jumping into a rushing river to save someone who can't swim. It took us two weeks to get back to a semblance of normal—or to get "down" from where we ended up during that trip in the national forest, surrounded by a pop-up village of weirdness. As the camp was being packed away and people were preparing to slip back into the night at the end of the gathering, Jim invited me to come back to Boulder, Colorado, with him. We hopped on his mid-'40s school bus he bought by pitching in with a group of other maniacs. They were inspired by *The Electric Kool-Aid Acid Test*, Tom Wolfe's retelling of the legend of Ken Kesey and his Day-Glo band of pranksters. I myself had been treating that book like scripture for the last few years, so Jim and I connected almost immediately. You ever meet people who are lost pieces of your soul in disguise as a friend? They are their own being, but it seems as though, a long time ago, you entrusted them with the ability to unlock a new piece of the divine in you. Jim was one of those people for me, and I knew at a young age that you chased friendships like that. You walked them out, these relationships, because there are soul lessons there. This is all to say, it made sense to go to Boulder—a place I had never been in a state I had never seen.

No one pays attention to the lost and lonely, really, and if you are a teen, you are invisible to almost everyone. Except law enforcement. The truth is that I wasn't hard to spot, being Black in Boulder, Colorado, and that is where things started to take a more serious turn. In the summer of '94, I found a collective of like-minded people in Boulder, and we started to form a family. Jim had brought me around his circle of friends, and by the middle of the summer, I was sure I would never make better ones in my life. It's rare to know when you are in one of the golden ages of your life. I find I usually recognize them after they have passed; it is in retrospect that I realize I was living in the Kin-dom of God. But this summer, it was like we all knew; we all knew that we were in rare air with this group of gathered people. We reveled in it, and to this day, that summer holds some of the happiest memories of my life. From late-night poetry with weathered beats, to eating more LSD than any person really should, to driving up the Front Range to just to look over the world and know all was well. That was where I started to write seriously for the first time in my life, where I fell in love, where I started to blossom into the person I am today. It was also the summer I started to realize that I stand out in really white spaces. At least to the police. You see, half the kids hanging out in Downtown Boulder were like me—usually between the ages of fifteen and twenty-one and smoking a ton of pot. Tripping and selling both to each other in a little cottage industry we had going on. We are not talking about sophisticated networks of a criminal enterprise that threatened the good people of Boulder. Nope, just a group of kids who like to smoke pot, sleep in the forest, and eat occasionally. Since I was sixteen the first time I was arrested—for selling a twenty-dollar bag of pot to an undercover—I was too old to be forced to go back home. I was a missing person, not a runaway. It also meant I had no community connections and was thrown into the byzantine maze of the juvenile justice system. A system where the rate of violence and particularly sexual violence, in my experience, is more

prevalent than its adult counterpart. The juvenile justice system is just the right amount of lack of rights and
feigned care for people that governments thrive on. You
fall in this gray area of society where you can't make decisions for yourself and need to be guided, and the public
knows that. But they don't give a fuck how that happens. It's an agreement made in the shadows of America.
We trust the local government to handle the "wayward
youth," and we pretend it's humane. America has made
all kinds of shadow agreements with you and me. We pretend we don't see the machinery of white supremacy and
that the machinery makes our life more comfortable. We
pretend not to hear the cries and screams of those being
ground up to power the system we all depend on. That's
the scary truth of the American story: you were in there
with me, and you don't even know it.

I was sent to Mount View Detention. This place is
still riddled with suicide and violence. Well, I was a smart-
ass and not indoctrinated into the prison politics thing. I
ended up in about four fights during my stay there. This
is a world where you intuitively know that any sign of
weakness will not be rewarded. I knew that every time
someone challenged me, I had to step up or I was going to
end up suffering one of the fates I saw other kids suffer.
Some of them in the same cell as their new tormentor or
rapist, too afraid to ask for a cell change because then it
would be open season on them. This is how this country
tried to help me because I sold about two joints' worth

of pot. Well, I was put in solitary. The way fights work, if you are like me, is that when the guard asks you what happened, you say nothing and you both get fourteen to thirty days in solitary. I was raised in a house where I was taught to say nothing to authorities.

During my first two-week stint in the hole, it was the lack of stimuli that shocked me. The way time starts to expand and contract with your state of mind. How your internal clock becomes attuned to when the door slit opens. Your plate of slop is dropped there. The slot is toward your kneecaps if you are standing, but you end up on the ground, looking up and out of it just to see something. Anything. The rattle of the guards' keys when they are on their rounds. The second time I ended up in there, it was thirty days. This felt different ten days in. There was nothing to look forward to, and I don't mean each day—it felt like there would *never* be anything to look forward to ever again, and I began to feel despair in a way that my young psyche had never felt before. I begged the guard for books, and he would only bring me one series: the entire Left Behind series, an evangelical fever dream about the end of the world, the rapture, and the antichrist. Great literature to read as your mind buckles.

The next visit was for sixty days. By this time, the direness of the situation was clear to me. I was going to be undone by this pattern of being alone and losing the ability to be among people. When I was again released into general, I stood out as a likely victim. My intuitive sense

of socializing was so warped and damaged that an altercation was a foregone conclusion in this environment. I
had to defend myself. Back to isolation.

There is a place deep down in the human soul that
few get to visit. It is the place where your internal dia-
logue, the narrator in your head, runs out of words. It
goes silent, but not in the way that enlightenment promises. It is not a harmonizing of the spheres so that you find
the silence of peace. No, this is as if your inner voice has
been snuffed out because right before it went quiet, it was
screaming. It was screaming about every wrong turn that
brought you to this place. It was ranting and raging about
your parents again and whispering desperate dreams of a
better tomorrow just right around the corner, just a little
bit further on. Your inner voice's throat was raw from all
that it screams into the void, and then it was cut off. As if
the hands of something more sinister had slipped over its
mouth, and the silence, the silence is so loud, it threatens
to end you. This is what it was like to be sixteen in solitary. This is the America I know. This is how you tried
to save me. A ton of my friends were doing the things I
was at that time in Boulder. But I was the only Black kid
in a circle of a few hundred. I had dreads, an East Coast
accent, and no one who cared about me with any power
in the situation. I was exposed to this torture as a child
for selling pot in a state where today it's totally legal.
Where rich white investors are now living off a feeding
frenzy of revenue. And a few very kind grower friends of

mine. In a lot of ways, everything I ever needed to know about America I learned reading the Left Behind series in solitary confinement when I was sixteen. That I was going to be alone in my struggle against white supremacy, and the most treasured dream of white Protestant America was to leave us all behind to the apocalypse because they "played by the rules."

9

THE ABSURDITY OF ADULTHOOD

Beloved, as you can tell by this point in my story, my formative years may not exactly match up with yours. Think, for example, of the things that stuck with you, the important lessons of your life: the mentor who got you through the first few years of college and beyond to graduation. The advice your father gave you before your first child was born. The wisdom of your mother that after years finally sunk deeply into who you are—like bone deep—and became a part of who you are. That stuff. I got zero of that going on. I mean, really. My mentors were sex workers, train hoppers, and dharma bums, and I have to tell you, in a lot of ways, I'm better for it. I was born to Leonard and Loretta Duncan, and they reared me until I was twelve. But the world raised me to adulthood, or a reasonable approximation of it. A cast of thousands went into my perspective, and for that, I will always be grateful. But it didn't always serve me so well, to be frank, especially not at first.

You see, I lived in a world that had been completely rejected by and yet still lived alongside society. It wasn't a seamless transition between these worlds, the one I had found out of survival and the one the rest of America I assumed enjoyed. They had gone to war for it, killed for it, and in the years after 9/11, happily traded away freedom for it. I had to assume it was enjoyable, and in a way, it was desirable to me. The idea that I could have my slice of the American pie, my own American story. I still believed, even after all I saw, in the so-called American dream. Full of hope and promise, I imagined that someday I would rise up like a swelling overture, and the notes of what I had seen and done would flood the world. That my writing or what I considered my wit would help me rise above the lot I was dealt in life and that this grand thing we have given so much for, America, would grant me its boon. I believed in this country in the way only the broken can. It takes all the faith in the American dream to be stripped away from you before you can really understand it. Only when you see the macabre and intricate system in its grotesque naked form do you really know what it is, or rather what it could be. To get that perspective, you have to get your ass kicked by this country. It has to be whipping your ass almost from day one. It has to have bruised you—and I mean young—in order for you to see what it has truly become.

But I also still believed, and believe now, in the promise of what America could be. What we could be if we but

tried. By the time I turned eighteen, I was finally looking up from my circumstances and could feel the tug of
something better. Something larger, a calling to be better,
and that by trying to be better, I would make the world
better. This was the first time I began to see community
and rootedness as being important. These are two things
that I still chase to this day, because I seem to be designed
by God not to naturally understand how to live or function in community. Maybe you are the same way? Maybe
you struggle with this whole walking among the people
thing. I know I do. As for rootedness, I had been a wild
seed blowing on the wind for too long to even imagine
what a rooted and centered holy life could look like. I say
holy because I now understand the sacredness of having,
knowing, and honoring your roots. I spent so much of
my time as a runaway trying to separate myself from my
roots because I was so concerned that I was rooted in
something poisonous. It would be decades until I realized
that my roots—my contextual uniqueness and particular social location—could be a gift to share. That I was
handcrafted to be the way I am by a loving design within
the larger architecture of a universe full of mystery and
joy. It is by examining my roots that I have become rooted
again. It is by going back that I am even able to fathom a
way forward for my life today.

At eighteen, I wasn't prepared for anything. To put
this in perspective, in 1997, I hadn't even owned a social
security card. I had only interacted with "society" when I

experienced the prison-industrial complex—not just my time in Mount View Detention but through the patchwork network of group homes, juvenile prisons, and faith-based programs that were really evangelical brainwashing factories sold as rehabilitation. Not to disparage the good people who served in these spaces during these years and the sacrifices they made, but honestly, if you are one of those people, I just want to wish you a hearty fuck you. That's a message from sixteen-year-old Lenny. A kid who was criminalized for running from an abusive home and was drawn ever closer to America's postmodern plantation network, commonly called the prison system. I was a kid who would have rather slept on the sidewalk at thirteen than go home, and you never once paused your murderous machine of justice to ask why. Why was this Black kid in Boulder, Colorado, sleeping on the streets? The only redeeming moments came from those who recognized the system for what it was, never bullshitted me, and gritted their teeth and tried to help me anyway. Still worked within its constraints but tried to help me break free. These were the one thousand points of light we had heard so much about, shining in those people who noticed me along the way. But the entire system seemed to be perfectly positioned so the American president who had waxed philosophical on that very notion would never see them.

At eighteen, I was lost. I had decided to come home for a little bit. I had a vague notion of heading to South

America to join some expat community, not even fathoming the amount of privilege it would take to pull that off. So I headed back to Philadelphia for a bit to stay with my parents and just be in Philadelphia. I was seeking rootedness. My parents had moved up the street to an apartment in Overbrook Park, the neighborhood next to ours. Just a mile away but a completely different world from the one I left behind six years earlier. Overbrook Park still had at the time a thriving enough Jewish community that kids could go sukkah hopping. More than enough Italian social clubs that every kid I met seemed to belong to one. And a thriving Black community that had moved from West Philly proper to Overbrook Park. It was West Philly at its finest in a lot of ways. Big homes, working-class families, and still enough of the city that it didn't feel like you weren't in it. Other areas close by like Upper Darby offered the same feel, but in those places, it was obvious you were no longer in Philadelphia. I don't know how to describe it to you; there is a grit and connectedness in Philadelphia that instantly fades away the minute you are outside its borders. Even by a couple of blocks. Overbrook Park, still well within the westernmost reaches of the city limit, was only about ten blocks from where I grew up, but you wouldn't know it. Cities on the East Coast make the socioeconomic lines and boundaries in the country so apparent, one would have to be stark raving mad not to see it. Every ten blocks, the culture, demographics, economic location, and level of access can vary wildly. Even when communities are reacting to abject poverty that is clearly designed by policy, there is rich diversity in resilience and resistance. If you asked at the time, circa 1997 to 1998, how Black people and people of color were expressing resistance in Overbrook Park, I would have answered simply, "With respectability." Weaponized respectability had long been a tactic of surviving America. Taking the tools of the very thing that is out to destroy you and mastering them. Showing how easily you have conquered the system designed to never let you win. It is a survival technique demonstrated by our ancestors and elders and originally turned into an art form by our legends in the civil rights era. It is clearly not the path that I have chosen, one of respectability, but I understand that without it, Black culture as I know it wouldn't exist, and we might still be living under strict Jim Crow inequality. Overbrook Park had turned to this technique of collective resistance—at least in my perspective as a kid from Sixty-Third Street, at the bottom of the hill—figuratively and literally. Manicured lawns and Black fraternity and sorority culture everywhere. This wasn't a bad thing; it was just a world I never engaged in but had a deep and abiding respect for and felt some jealousy toward. Before I left home at thirteen, I was on the fast track to any college I wanted. Education was the weapon I chose to survive in America at first. In a different timeline, I would have gone off to an HBCU, and who knows who I would have been? Or at least this is the story I would tell myself. But I understood that intellect was something America didn't expect from me as a young Black child and that it was the only thing I was armed with. Lowered expectations and a keen sense for what academia was asking of me, not necessarily a call to academics as an institution, had served me well. My point is, I knew survival when I saw it, and I knew thriving in revolution when I saw it.

So I saw the flowerbeds on our new block for what they were: strategic defense. The BBQ patio arranged with military precision, the well-waxed car out front—these were all a frontline defense against white supremacy. Many in my community arranged themselves in these sorts of configurations, and a lot of them thrived. Hell, a lot of them were my heroes. It was good to be home too. I had missed my brother's last visit with my parents. Since I had chosen to live an "alternative lifestyle," as folks were calling it at the time, Daniel had been assailed and captured by the criminal justice system. Still a juvenile in the eyes of the law but already categorized and targeted by the prison-industrial complex in a way I don't think I will ever understand. Since I had been gone, Danny had three several-month stints, was sent home, and then after violating some rule, was placed back in custody. The latest time had ruined any chance my family had at respectability on the new block.

My parents decided to take a few days "down the shore." "Down the shore" is a whole way of life in the tristate area. Weekend to weeklong excursions to Atlantic City or Ventnor Beach had been a ritual in my family passed on by our grandfather. Edward rented a little shore house in Atlantic City every summer, and we loaded three generations in three cars to go and just be on the beach. We would use it as a home base for Wildwood, New Jersey, excursions. Wildwood stands as South Jersey's gem of boardwalk culture, only eclipsed by the storied history of Asbury Park farther north. My parents had hardly ever been able to afford to do one of these little trips together, and despite what I have already shared with you, they loved each other. Through my father's complicated battle with substances, his childhood trauma, and his own abuse, which he turned around and perpetrated on the people he loved. Through the overtly problematic relationship my mother had with his love, which she could bask in, and her troubling framework of what marriage, fidelity, and God all meant for her. Despite her own deep scars, recognized and unrecognized, somehow they loved each other. The relationship between the abused and the abuser is complicated enough to navigate, but consider this: I still loved my father then and still do to this day. My parents still loved each other like the first day they met. I'm saying that people are complicated, and so is love. Here I was at home, and my parents were making a go of it, and I was honestly happy for them.

But back to the destruction of respectability in the Duncan home in Overbrook Park. So my parents went on this trip *down the shore* the weekend before I got home. Danny stayed home, like most sixteen-year-olds are apt to do, and started planning a series of parties. I mean, it's exactly what I would have done. Well, one of these get-togethers got out of hand, and Danny got in an altercation. Somewhere in the mix, there was a gun, but it was just mostly a scuffle between kids. This sort of escalation was becoming very common in the city at the time. In this case, there was no gun violence, only the threat of it. Due to terrorism, gun culture has perpetrated person-of-color communities, and I don't want to make light of it. But this sort of thing has been happening my entire life in my neighborhood. I mean, one of the first things Danny and I found exploring as kids in a new apartment near Fifty-Second Street in West Philly was a sawed-off shotgun. Guns had been pouring into our neighborhood for decades, and we weren't the ones manufacturing them or allowing a large part of the populace ready access to them. What I'm trying to convey to you is that this thing that happened wasn't a big deal in the grand scheme of the neighborhood, but it became one quickly.

Someone called the police and told them that Danny assaulted them and was holed up in the house with a gun. I don't know what happened—I wasn't there—but I know no gun was ever found. I know they blocked off the street and tried to talk Danny out of the house. I know they positioned officers to block the back alley. I know they eventually kicked in the door and stormed the house. I know that my brother had sneaked out thirty-five minutes earlier. I know my father's aquarium was broken, which for him was the biggest problem with this scenario. I know that two days after this happened, my parents came home to police tape on the door and no explanation. I know they walked into a wrecked house from a hasty police search. I know Danny was arrested for a probation violation a few days later and never charged with anything related to this incident. I know he never had a fucking shot.

This is where I landed a week later. This is the home I walked into and the parents I met. I had gone years without even speaking to them, but I asked my mom if I could come home and rest my weary bones. I had been rambling so damn long, I just needed to stop for a second to either catch up with the rotation of the earth or let it catch up with me. I had been spending the last five years really pushing the levels of my sanity with psychedelics and chasing spiritual experiences across the country. From drinking dozens of peyote buttons at a time to eating acid like it was my job every morning for several summers. Honestly, I was fried, dyed, and laid to the side, if you are picking up what I'm putting down. I needed some respite, and my family (read: my mother) offered it to me. My mother and I had developed a loving but strange relationship over the last few years. Sometimes I would get stopped by a cop, and they would eventually get my mom on the phone. That tends to happen as a thirteen-year-old street urchin. I would get on the phone and promise to come home if she would authorize them to release me. They would put me on a Greyhound bus with a sack lunch and make me promise not to come back to their county. This happened to me at least a dozen times. This is how your local sheriff would deal with kids like me. After sixteen, I wasn't even a runaway; I was just a missing person. But for years, I would lie to my mother, who for her part wanted me home desperately but also understood what I was running from. But I still broke her heart dozens of times. I'm not proud of this, but I have to acknowledge how much the first woman in my life loved me and how I took advantage of that. That I'm not the hero in this story. That I am just as messy, complicated, lost, and alone as the next person.

For me, family is messy and complicated. This is the home, heartache, and hope that I walked into in an attempt to try to be an adult. I went back to my roots. It is here that the seeds of the great joys of my life would be planted. This is the time where I started to stretch myself a little more, where my own battles with substances started to scare me, and I realized surviving my teens wasn't the end but the beginning of a much longer journey in this world. It was 1997, and I was back in Philly.

10

THE DAY I MET MY DAUGHTER

I was so incredibly nervous, I could feel the wetness of my palms and the flush red-hot shame starting to rise up on my face and into my spirit. I was seated in a railcar speeding out to the Philadelphia suburb of Aston. My head was racing with blurred scenes from the last thirteen years. Each memory chasing me, hunting me in my despair, and pinning me against the walls of my own mounting failures. I was on my way to meet the daughter I hadn't seen in twelve years, not since she was just a little over a year old.

It was 2012, and I had spent the last few years cleaning up my act. Whatever that means. At the time, my spiritual home was a twelve-step program, and part of the deal was that I had to mend my fences or clean up the wreckage of my past. So I had spent the last year or so trying to restore what I had stolen from people who had the misfortune of running across me at my worst.

Substance abuse and drinking in particular had crippled me for the last decade, and it led to a series of arrests and the ever more dangerous prospect of the prison-industrial complex becoming my permanent home and place in society. One of the insidious things about the criminal justice system is that it thrives on instability. I mean, it is the stuff it gorges on: Moved away and missed a notice via snail mail? Violation. Lost your job and missed a payment or a fine? Violation. Can't pull yourself up by your bootstraps in twenty-eight days and conform to a confusing and impossible set of social rules? Violation.

And look, I don't want to pretend that there weren't times that I threw myself headlong into the abyss. In my brokenness, I had done things like heroin for a year on a lark. I had sat up for days trying to shoot enough meth to make my heart burst. I had found some of the rough and razor-edge places in this world, walked to the very edge of the blade, and tried to jump off. So I don't want to pretend that I was always the hero of this story. There were plenty of times where drinking had turned me into the villain of someone else's narrative. I had gone from a delight that danced through your life to an unnatural disaster that ripped through things you held precious and left you to pick up the shattered pieces.

At various points in our stories and lives, we can be both hero and villain in the lives of others. Take your own life, for example. In some people's stories, you are one of the very things that prove that God is real. You're one of the things that prove that there is design to this world and universe. You are a sign of life and resurrection in that person's story and one of the plot threads that ties to their very salvation.

In another person's story, you have been at best a disruptive rhythm or stray path best left behind as a lesson learned but not revisited. In another's story, you are the corrosive thread running through their heartache and tied to their deep-soul trauma. You are, either rightly or wrongly, the bad actor in their narrative who went about the intentional and heinous act of hurting them. We wound, often deeply, those around us, and even if we are aware and repentant, it doesn't change one thing. You have broken something. My friend Nadia is a pastor, and she says you can tell the big stuff, the covenant-like stuff, when it's violated. You know when you have transgressed those boundaries, those fundamental "rules" of spirituality, for lack of a better term, because what you have broken can't be fixed. This relationship is shattered. It is lying there, and the cracks that have occurred are irreparable. That's who you are to some people out there.

But in my case, I have done an inordinate amount of this sort of damage in people's lives. I was starting to realize that if there was a cosmic ledger balance, it was never going to be nil. On this day, on this train to Delaware County from my apartment in the Northern Liberties section of Philadelphia, although I was utterly convinced of the graciousness of the Divine, I also knew

I could spend my whole life giving back to the world, and it wouldn't be enough.

I had become convinced in the way only grace could ever convince anyone. I had become convinced that no matter what, I needed to spend the rest of my life pouring it out for others. It's hard to explain what happened to me in the time since I heard that voice telling me I was getting sober. I would have told you on that train headed out to meet my daughter that that moment was me hitting my bottom. That I had just had enough, that I had reached the end of my rope. Now when I look back on that day in 2010 and on this scene of me in 2012 hurtling toward perhaps the greatest moment of my life, I would say that the truth is much more mysterious than just "a broken man gets his shit together."

The thing I have been trying to tell you is that there seems to be some force in the universe—I call it Grace or God, but whatever it is for you is cool with me—that is highly interested in our little human lives. It seems to be more than interested; it steps into space and time for the purpose of salvation. For the purpose of saving our collective asses. For the cause of liberation and freedom. And this thing, this being, this God has been acting in my own life and saved it. I am not here to tell you what framework or tradition or path you should take to find this thing I'm trying to tell you about. Nor do I privilege my own way or language of describing this shared human experience. I am simply saying the Divine is real and has intervened in my life. This day. This train ride I'm about to tell you about. It is the testament in my own life.

You have testaments written in the blood and tears of your own life. You have things that shout glad tidings to your soul, and these things, these moments, these places in your story, they are what keep you nourished and thriving. They are touchstones and inner compasses. They are creased and folded road maps of your own journey and path through this world. They are sacred, holy, and rare.

On this day, I was screaming down the tracks toward one of these moments, and I was keenly aware of it. I think that's what makes some moments more formative then others in our lives. There are ones where you are consciously aware that something big is happening. Fate-altering stuff. Moments when you can sense the nearness of God—or perhaps the nearness of life, of resurrection, of the perfect order of the cosmos being momentarily clear. The harmonies of the celestial spheres themselves coming into tune all on one note that, for one brief second, you hear straining over the hills. Those moments. I was headed for one.

In 1998, while I was back in Philly, I had met a girl named Bree. She was lovely and sweet and came from, judging by all the typical markers, a good home—which meant that we might as well have come from different universes. Brown hair and a tentative smile, she was all baggy pants and ugly sweaters. Grandpa button-downs and Chuck Taylors. Teen angst wrapped in evangelical theology and strained through the lens of faux rebellion. She had the most beautiful eyes I had ever seen. They were brown mirrors that gave a soft, empathic reflection to the most treasured parts of yourself. I hadn't seen the gentle parts of me reflected in the gentle parts of someone else in so long that I knew it was something to be treasured. Something to be pursued and chased, even. Bree was hauntingly easy in her approach to the world and could enter a scene so quietly that you didn't know she was there until you were already talking with her. She had an easy disposition and would listen to others in a way that conveyed the absolute conviction that this was someone who could hear you. She was obsessed with the lyrics and poetry of Dylan and still thought the church was an important community. In my overly juvenile and traumatized way, I could only deal in absolutes. The nuanced way that she approached subculture, music, and her faith life was something I had never seen before. That a person could follow a church and still smoke pot, listen to cool music, and talk to me about leftist thought was mind blowing to me. In the years since, Bree has struggled with her faith, and it has changed radically since that time, but what she doesn't know is that she is the first Christian I ever met that I believed. Who seemed sincere and was living it out. Not in a shitty way like when I announce I am Christian and then publicly pantomime kindness as some form of "evangelism." Fuck that inauthentic garbage that never worked and never will. It amazes me that Christians of all stripes haven't given up that stuff already.

No, Bree was a Christian. You knew that, although she was Jewish by descent and heritage. She was amazing to be around. She was full of wonder and kindness. She was like experiencing the world all over again. She had one of the sharpest senses of sarcasm I heard in someone so young. But that was it. And I can't tell you how powerfully influential it was that, for the rest of my life, when I would imagine what a "good Christian" was, it was Bree. She never invited me to her wild-ass evangelical community, and I never shit on her beliefs. Maybe it was because I saw her in action when no one was looking. I saw her compassion and empathy play out in our day-to-day lives in Overbrook Park. I was living with my parents and working at a local gas station. You remember in the last chapter, when I didn't ping-pong you around two decades?

That's when I met her. I was so afraid and ashamed in so many ways about who I was, what I had done, who I was becoming. You ever wonder about the movie of your life? Like what would it be? Maybe your life is a redemption story. Or it could be a story of tragedy. Maybe it is a high drama or a political thriller. Up until I met Bree, I had hoped mine was like a teen '80s comedy movie. You know the type, like *Better off Dead*, *Wet Hot American Summer*, or even *Animal House*, minus the rape culture and whiteness. But when I met Bree, I suddenly imagined it could be a love story. Y'all, I tried in my nineteen-year-old way to fit into "neighborhood" culture and be what this group of folks perceived to be a boyfriend. My instincts were telling me that since we were together and we loved each other, we should hit the road together. But apparently, she liked her family and her home or some bullshit. My friend Jason introduced us. I met Jason because he was walking down the street, and I could tell he smoked pot. That was it; that was my sole qualification for friendship at the time. I asked if he wanted to get stoned, and he said yes. We had been partying for two months before I met Bree. He played guitar, his friend Eric played bass, and I wrote poetry. We hung in Jason's basement so much, I ended up moving in at one point. Bree and I spent a few months together, and by this time, things shifted. By this time, my insecurities showed up. By this time, the trauma of my childhood abuse convinced me she didn't really like me anyway. By this time, I became convinced she was just as untrustworthy as everyone else that had tried to love me. By this time, those voices had won a battle in an internal war that I would have to keep fighting for decades.

There was a war raging inside me, and it was a battle between nothing less than death and life. Death was always trying to convince me that I had no inherent worth, that I wasn't imbued with something so incredibly wonderful. Just like you are. The job of death is to

convince diamonds they are coals and stars in the sky that
they are a dime a dozen. And I wasn't someone who could
choose life. I never could adhere to life-giving paths or
start to build a rich and full world for myself. I was having
too much fun just surviving. *I couldn't imagine a life beyond
just surviving.*

By the time I lost that battle, I was already being cruel
and awful to Bree. By the time I had started the pattern
that would haunt for me for years to come, she was pregnant. She came to tell me in the middle of a thunderstorm
that turned the sky pitch black and shook the windows
with each thunderbolt. It was the '90s, so to find me, she
had to bounce from house to house, calling around to
try to track me down in the neighborhood. I opened the
door when she knocked, and she stood there with soaked
dark hair and the face of a wounded angel and outlined
by flashes in the sky. She said, "I'm pregnant."

We weren't together. And then we were. We tried.
I mean, we were two teenagers from two completely different universes having a child. Bree grew up with two
ex-Jesus-movement parents who were now attending a
messianic synagogue. Her father, David, was everything
I had ever wanted in a father, and I remember being so
ashamed of that. Like red-hot rage in my face that this
white man stoked such a need for affection and approval.
Such hunger for love. He was just good. I didn't know
fathers could be "just good." Her mother, Sharon, engen-
dered the same visceral shame in me. When I looked at

Sharon, I saw all the opportunities my mom was denied by the world, while Sharon simply was free enough to just fuss over knickknacks in the dining room. She was protective of Bree, particularly from me, and I don't blame her. I was completely up to no fucking good in life. And I had just got their daughter pregnant. Their daughter who was supposed to be at the youth group at church and instead was hanging out with me. Bree had been doing that sort of thing for years before she met me, but I certainly was the consequence of that behavior in Sharon's mind. Sharon was sweet and prayerful. The daughter of a missionary with generations of pastors in her line dating back to the 1800s and influential in the founding of the Assemblies of God.

I'm pretty sure Loretta got extra drunk one day just to work up the courage to get on the phone with Sharon during that time, so you know these families were going to get along great. Around that time, I got arrested for selling LSD at a local festival because I couldn't imagine another way to get financially stable. I ended up getting eleven and a half to twenty-three months in Montgomery County Jail for the sale of three hits of acid. That's where I was when I found out that my first child had been born.

I was on the top bunk as the night pushed toward the early dawn hours. I had started to experience the often months-long bouts of insomnia that only a year or more in jail can start to really afflict you with. I had worked my way to the kitchen pod so I wouldn't starve. One of the grossest consequences of the marriage between capitalism and the prison-industrial complex is that if you don't have family sending you money, you won't even get enough food to survive. Just enough food to keep you weak and unable to give the guards trouble. No soap. I mean, once every two weeks, they hurl a hotel bar at you, but that's it. It's bleak, but I had somehow had enough "good behavior" to work in the kitchen. This meant that I could avoid the rampant violence and fights you mostly have no control over. I had just arrived at that unit or pod or cell block the day before. I could work in the kitchen twelve hours a day for a decent meal, basically. Also five bucks a week. Soap! I was the new guy, so I got top bunk right under the so-called emergency light. I lay on top of the itchy blanket listening to the jangle of a guard's keys as they slowly made their way around from cell to cell. I heard the sound of mail sliding under the door. I figured it was my celly's and jumped down to put it on our shared desk for him.

Have you ever been in a "modern" county jail cell? It is the size of the average American bathroom with two people, a sink, a toilet, and a desk with a bunk bed. I landed lightly on my bare feet and picked up the letter and saw that it was addressed to me. At the time, the only person who wrote was my mom, and it was, at best, sporadic. She was devoted to my brother and his problems almost solely. I never begrudged her this; I was scrappy and would make it. There was an unspoken exchange between us when I was a teen and a runaway that she had enough to survive with my father and trying to love and protect my brother. I had struck out on my own, and as much as it broke her heart, she respected my choice. I also suspected her drug use was out of control. People were coming in and out of the jail with stories of the Kensington neighborhood in Philly morphing into an open-air drug market with the strongest heroin seen in a generation. Her letters were becoming fewer and further between. I jumped back up to my bunk and opened it. It was a handmade card with the incredible cursive flourishes that only a Catholic education in the mid-'70s in Pennsylvania can give you. And written in huge letters, covered in glitter, and colored in for effect were three words: "It's a girl."

Under it was written simply, "And her name is Jenna Marie." I sat under the low fluorescent emergency light that created a halo around those words and enshrined them in my memory. In that moment, the biological instinct to hold my daughter was so strong that it felt like my body seized up. I mean, the visceral need to have her in my arms was so incredibly strong that I could have screamed for hours and it wouldn't have been enough to sate the need. That was how I learned the name of my daughter. That she was real. That she was born. She was here. That her name was Jenna. It was in that moment that I knew I had become everything I ran away from. A deadbeat, abusive, drug-addled father. My self-contempt threatened to smother me in my sleep the next night.

When I got out, Bree and I tried. We moved in with my parents, who were now back on Sixty-Third Street living above my grandparents. We had fun, I had a little job, and we were trying to be parents, even though we had no idea what that meant. Bree, I suspected, was more interested in my parents' lack of regard for rules or social mores. Her parents had understandably been influenced by the late-'90s megachurch version of draconian "tough love." We were young, and I don't fault Bree for not understanding the socioeconomic and cultural differences that could exist just by living two miles away. I mean, my parents lived fifteen minutes from hers. It was the first time we stole diapers and formula together that I knew things wouldn't work. Not because she didn't love me or I didn't love her or because we couldn't have found a way to make it work. But because we both knew she deserved better and her parents could provide better. Jenna was under two and just a ball of joy and laughter. Jenna was utterly devastating in her beauty and carried a smile that could cut your heart to ribbons. She still had that fresh-baby smell. The smell of preciousness and promise, of futures undecided and fates still being written. I wanted that open future for her desperately.

The plan was that I would return to Colorado, stay with my friend Jim, and get a job and a little apartment for Bree and Jenna to join me. Bree would move back in with her parents for a few months. My parents' darker days of heroin use were slowly starting to swallow them whole. I was starting to realize this situation was dangerous, even if Bree wasn't aware. Bree's dad, David, was enthusiastic and helpful. Looking back now, I see it was a win-win for him. Either I would be successful and huzzah for the new family, or I would fall on my face. Either way, it got his daughter and granddaughter out of West Philly.

But a corrosive secret was starting to slowly eat its way into any sense of self I had left. I wouldn't be able to pull this off. This dad thing. This going-to-Colorado-and-setting-up-the-foundation-for-a-new-life thing. I was capable of keeping a job and paying rent. Making friendships and building a life. I mean, with a ton of extracurriculars, but I could do it. But stringing all that together in a deep relationship with another human being and raising and protecting a child? Maybe I could find love, but my home, my story, my roots are too infected with generational brokenness and abuse to raise a child. I would sit up all night asking whatever was out there to not make me like my father. Begging the universe to break the cycles of trauma and pain. Fevered prayers fueled by that deep shame I felt on the top bunk in jail. "Please, please, don't ever let me lay a hand on my child or Bree. Please don't let me be a deadbeat. Please let me provide. Please teach me to be good." I mean, this was a constant, obsessive fear. I know now that this was a perfectly reasonable response to living in the home of the main perpetrator of my abuse with my own child, but at the time, I had no idea why I was heart stricken with these thoughts.

I didn't feel worthy of love. Worthy of being a father.

I could feel the weight of these thoughts beginning to smother me, and I knew in a secret place deep down inside that I would give in to my shadow patterns of substance abuse and escape. That's the secret in this story. I'm not a victim. I was aware of all I was up against, all the systemic brokenness stacked against me; I was aware I was being presented with an opportunity to change my family's story. I also knew I would fuck it up. That I would burn it all down, given enough pushback from the world. Just the right amount of resistance in a situation that by any measure was tough, and I would collapse, I would implode, I would be nothing but the dust of failure that mushrooms up when the very structures of our lives fall down around us. I knew I would be standing there covered in shame and regret.

And I was OK with it.

I had never felt more broken or out of options. The inevitable happened. I went to Colorado, and things were good at first. Then things were hard. Someone offered me some drugs. I melted away into America.

Twelve years later, as I hurtled toward this daughter I hadn't seen since then, I was flustered. I had thought of her every day since and had never felt worthy enough to be in her life. But on this day, I was armed with a universal truth. No one is worthy of love. None of us. The great thing about love is precisely that we aren't worthy of it. We don't have to earn it or be made ready on the altar of perfection to receive it. Or give it. That last part was the trickiest on this day. Because I had no right to give love or share my love with this thirteen-year-old girl I was going to meet. But I wanted to share it because it had been burning in my heart for over a decade, and I couldn't wait to meet her. I also knew something else.

I was not there to fix what was broken because it can't be fixed. What I did to Jenna and to Bree. Those are things that can only be cleaned up through repentance and the hopes of reparation—through giving something back of value and worth to add to their lives now. But that stuff will never be fixed or made the way it was, or could have been, or should have been.

On the day I met my daughter, I knew all this deep down in my bones as I stood up to get off the train. I could tell you about sitting down with her that afternoon. It had been a year since I had a similar conversation with Bree. We had planned and cultivated this afternoon, father and daughter, for months prior. I could describe in detail how I asked my beautiful thirteen-year-old daughter how I could make this right. Her response. But frankly, her perception of this moment in time is probably so incredibly different than my own. It doesn't feel like my story. It feels like our story and thus isn't "mine" to tell.

I *can* tell you about what has happened in the years since. Since that day, I have learned to be a father. Not the greatest, but Jenna has told me I am the only man she has ever respected. I'll take that. On our best days, I just feel lucky to be her friend. She has a wit and grace wrapped in an intense level of compassion for the world and everyone in it that is astounding. Bree and I got married. I guess somewhere in the course of watching me being a father, she started to have feelings for me. For my part, I had always held a torch for Bree all these years but was afraid that if I opened myself to love, I would hurt Bree or Jenna again. That, quite frankly, the worst parts of me would show up. But remember those emphatic brown eyes that reflected the gentlest part of me? I could see myself being a good man in her eyes, and I liked that. We were married on April Fool's Day in 2013. In her parents' living room. My parents were present too.

It's hard to explain the power of Grace. It's hard to pin down the elusive moments that string together over decades and create a providential series of events that somehow resurrect stolen fates and lives. It's hard to explain the evidence of Grace in your life. To create a patchwork tapestry weaved together of stolen moments in your life that seem to be urging you into a new pattern. One that stitches life into the very fabric of reality. To present that for public examination and speculation. That's not an easy thing to do. But you know it's there in your own story. You know those places, and you point to them all the time. I'm pointing to one of mine. The day I met my daughter, that's one of mine. It's my evidence that God is real.

11

STAINED GLASS SHELTER
FROM THE STORM

It was late summer 2015, and I had no fucking idea what I was doing. I sat in the back of a large converted cafeteria area in the Brossman Center of the Lutheran Theological Seminary at Philadelphia and had no idea why I was there. Like, intellectually, I knew that for the last few years, I had been exploring what Christians term a "call to ministry," which is a very benign way to describe what I had been experiencing since that day in 2010 at the back of the show where we started this story. I encountered this strange Christ, and the trajectory of my life was altered by the trajectory of Grace. Because since that day, it has felt like Jesus has been hunting me in the streets like some sort of crazed maniac. I mean, it started subtle enough. A quiet drumbeat of strange ideas like *you should be a pastor* bubbling up from the deep well of my subconscious only to be easily defeated by the logic of the everyday that makes something like becoming a pastor seem ludicrous. I wasn't even part of a church at the time this started to grow in my heart. It was 2012 the first time I stayed up into the night arguing with God in prayer about just how fucking crazy God sounded. Screaming into dark rooms my refusal to serve a God I didn't want to get to know.

Pastor!?

I had barely admitted to myself that I was Christian. I was still sneaking around my partners or friends to go to church when no one was looking. You see, I didn't know much about this "following Jesus" thing, but I knew intuitively there was a difference between knowing that Christ had intervened in your life and *following him*. And I wanted no part of that bullshit. None. I mean, really, I had studied Scripture enough, and from what I could tell, it seemed like a shitty deal. This discipleship thing. Like, none of Jesus's first followers did well; they all had terrible endings according to folklore and church history. Hung upside down on crosses or torn to pieces by angry mobs. That was the top guys, the upper management. My point is, from what I could tell, postresurrection, the franchise opportunities have sucked.

And that is not even talking about the white supremacist tool of oppression the church has largely become in America. You don't live the kind of life that I have lived without developing some sort of power analysis of the world and its institutions. It was clear to me what

the church in North America was. What it had been com-
plicit in over the last four hundred years in this country.
How it was a tool of politicians and culture warriors to
cloak agendas with the false narrative of a nation founded
on Christian ideals. They would use this narrative to
serve whatever war on foreign soil they needed to feed
the economy. It was always the poor who lubricated this
war machine's wheels with blood at home and abroad.
These were the architects of the doctrine of discovery
who read a Bible to my ancestors that contained only
232 chapters (the standard Protestant Bible contains 1,200).
They did this so they could remove every reference to
rebellion, liberation, and a God who steps into human
history for the purpose of salvation here and now. *In
this life.* Who has changed the courses of empires to free
that same God's people. Slave owners must have feared
Moses more than Pharaoh ever did.

Yet here I was. Spending Saturday nights in the pews
of strange churches across the city and bursting into tears
thinking about how expansive and powerful God's love
is. I was not thrilled. Nothing seemed worse to me than
to have washed up on the shores of an institution that
I believed in my core had largely been the antithesis of
everything I knew to be true about the Divine. Let alone
what little I knew of the gospel narrative. And yet, in
my own life, I experienced God to be the very engine of
change and creativity. But that's not what I saw when I
was in the church. I enjoyed the forms and the patterns

of worship, but the people around me sure didn't seem like they did. A lot of them seemed to be sleepwalking through the service or really freaked out by me waving my tatted arms excitedly upfront. Most seemed non-plussed by anything happening in church or the stories being told. But I didn't blame the people for that.

It was almost like a lot of the pastors I ran into were reading a completely different Bible than the one I stole from their church. I mean, this book seemed subversive and full of ideas that would be enough to get you arrested for treason in most industrialized countries. Yet they tended to use it to either rein in people's passion and desires or create entire systems of false morality to imprison folks' genitalia. If it was a more "progressive" church, I would listen to pastors obtusely poke around issues of justice with the indifference of a five-year-old poking a jellyfish on the beach with a stick.

Or sometimes on Saturday night, I would wander into an evangelical nondenominational praise service. They seemed almost too happy to be there, and the casual way they would mix oppression into the proclamation or exclusion into even the way they did welcome was troubling. But at least it wasn't as dreary as a mainline church. Those fucking ministers sounded like they all had some weird version of progressive theological Stockholm syndrome. Like reluctant prisoners to the promises of the gospel, they weren't really on board with liberation at all. Instead, they were captured by the gravity of the church and the twenty-first century and were suddenly trying to learn pronouns.

I knew one thing throughout all this wrestling with God. The last thing I would let Jesus do to me is force me to become one of those lame, dreary, robe-wearing priests who read the words of institution like ingredients from a soup can every worship. I mean, their main thing was communion, which centers on a moment called the *words of institution*. Fuck your institutions.

But despite all that, in 2015, I found myself sitting in the back of a converted cafeteria area at the Lutheran Theological Seminary at Philadelphia. I had no fucking idea what I was doing. If you saw me, I would probably have looked like I was about to be lined up against the wall and shot. Everyone else around me was very excited about this "discernment" weekend. It was called Wet Toes Weekend, and it was nowhere as kinky as advertised by the name. I wanted to die from embarrassment before I even went.

Everything on campus has a name. They gave us a tour, and the entire building was dedicated to donors. It's decadent in the way that only academia when married with capitalism can be—public displays of affection in bronze, and the seminary fucking hangs them everywhere. I would later learn this is a Lutheran thing. A little bronze plaque patting a forgotten family on the back for a donation that is just some line on a spreadsheet now.

I wasn't having a great day. I sat next to some blond kid and started making fun of the speaker. I kept rolling my eyes as the guy talked about "urban ministry" in Baltimore—which I assumed was code for "Black." I said out loud that this dude had no idea what he was talking about to the kid, and he was eating up every caustic observation and sarcastic takedown I threw the speaker's way. We laughed in the back the way only delinquents can when making fun of authority and its self-assuredness. The guy up front talking was the president of the school. The kid I was sharing my critique with was his son. Like I said, it wasn't a great day.

That "kid," Micah, would become a dear friend and would join a cast of characters who would become part of the story that is currently unfolding in my life. In fact, they are the very center of who I am today and my reason for being—or, rather, the thing I was put on this earth to do. But on this day, he just seemed like proof that I didn't belong, *a belonging that, by the way, I was desperate for.* I had spent the last few years desperately searching for any reason to walk away from this ministry thing I had started pursuing. It had taken a lot to go from a GED I had earned in 1998 in county jail just to get out of my cell in the morning to walking the halls of a graduate school. I had crammed a bachelor's degree into eighteen months, and somehow, Jesus had trapped me into what I assumed would be a pretty lame future. I mean, I had a good run and a lot of fun up to this point.

During those eighteen months, I had wandered into a Lutheran church and was invited to preach in a similar manner that I was invited to visit the seminary that day. You see, that church met me with a deep sense of curiosity and a radical sense of affirmation. An invitation to be in community together. The seminary was doing a similar dance with me. It was enticing in its movements and rhythms. It had already started to draw me in with its well-appointed hallways and stories of centuries-long traditions of forming leaders for the church. As lame as becoming a pastor sounded (and still sounds to my ears today), it was what was happening to me. Has happened to me. Is what I am, or what I was meant to be, or how things just turned out. To be honest, all three explanations work for me to try to explain the fickle way fate decides between life and death. The way you careen down the road of your life one way and then suddenly realize that tragedy can be narrowly averted. Has been averted. I believe that my life has been purposefully and carefully taken from a dead-end street and artfully placed on a new path that leads to life and love, handcrafted by an active Creator who also steps into space and time to do the same for you.

You see, that's why I was walking the hallways of the seminary listening to someone drone on about the undercroft of the library that day in the Mount Airy neighborhood in Philly. Love was real. It was alive, and it was active in human history. The twenty-five-year journey that took tens of thousands of miles; several countries; thousands of loves, friends, and heartbreaks.

That took a bruised and bloody twelve-year-old victim of abuse from one side of Philly, swept him up in grace disguised as youthful folly, and used the entire country and all the sharp, broken pieces of his story to move him almost directly across Philly. To an entirely different universe. One that was populated with mercy and incredibly great fucking people who would become the very reason I get up in the morning willing to fight. Willing to scream. Willing to wage peace on a world so desperate for war and conflict. You see, I was about to meet the people I would be in community *for* who would give me strength to deal with some of those I was in community *with*.

I was about to lose what I thought was God—or, more accurately, to have it deconstructed and handed back to me like some sort of Tinkertoy to put back together.

I was about to find my voice.

It's a funny thing when you find your voice. When you start to discover shared language in a community that is able to pinpoint your exact location in the cosmos, I mean really pin down where you are coming from, who you were created to be, and what this world may have in store for you. When you have a clarity of thought that can only come from finally finding the right divine frequency. It's like my muse had been screaming in my ear for decades at just below or above my hearing, and one day I got tuned in. Suddenly, the station screamed to life, and all I could do was type as fast as I could to get everything down. That experience a writer waits for their whole life. It is a finite resource that can descend upon creatives, and I believe it's proof that God not only is real but loves us.

That was about to happen in three months thanks to these hallways and these people I was sneering at. Not because of anything they did or perhaps who they were in particular, since God seems to deal in a strange form of particularity that leads to a door that everyone has the key for. But these folks, this place. It was the vehicle that helped me discover who I was born to be, and I am acutely aware of how fucking Pollyanna that sounds.

We wandered up the stairs past what seemed to be a hundred-foot-tall painting of the day Isaac realized his parents were the literal fucking worse, Abraham dumbstruck and knife falling out of his hand. The look of betrayal on Isaac's face. I wore that face a lot as a kid. When you know a parent can harm you, it makes a face you can wear, and this painting captured it in all its raw, gory detail. I had no idea why this was hung up at all, and as we strolled up the steps past it, Isaac looked at me from the painting and mouthed, "You don't belong here." I whispered back, "I know."

As we got near the top of the steps, I could tell the tour was winding down, which was fine with me. I started to map my escape route around Matt, the kind admissions guy in the bow tie who seemed to be having way too much fun, and the gaggle of excited folks around me. I stood in the back shifting between feelings of deep suspicion of this scene unfolding before me and incredible interest—it generated an earnestness that wanted to burst from my heart. I looked over Matt's shoulder and saw a Black depiction of Christ in wood right behind him. It was gorgeous and dark, and I wanted to get closer to it—to see *me* in the God who walked as a poor man from Nazareth, this God who was lynched by law enforcement and hung by the state from a tree. I rounded the crowd to get a better look, and it was there that the church defeated me. It was there that I knew I would serve the people who gathered in this strange way for the rest of my life.

At the foot of the cross that hot summer of 2015 was a small rack holding note cards and pictures. There against the wall for all to see but laid innocently and humbly enough were little white index cards, each scrawled with little notes and names. In different colors and wildly different handwritings that belayed this was a community effort, these were the prayers of the people.

They said names like Mike Brown. Clementa Pinckney. Trayvon Martin. Sandra Bland.

The notes said things like "Jesus screams #blacklivesmatter." There at the foot of the cross were handwritten prayers for reparations, revolution, reconciliation, and justice. Mixed with notes of grace and mercy. Prayers for finals and for ordinations. For the community and for friends and family who had died. There at the foot of the cross stood the trap that would slam down on me that day, the final spring triggered, and there I lay captured.

I knew I would do anything to be a part of a world that could imagine a God like this, one that would treat these martyrs the way they should be, lifted in our worship, surrounded in our prayers, outlined in our proclamation and outrage, a table where we could break ourselves open for the sake of the names laid at the foot of the cross. For the queer leaders whose bodies wrote those prayers and for an institution that made space for this.

I never had the courage to tell the queer Black woman who I later learned had organized that display that she saved my life that day.

Nor would I tell anyone of the secret face Isaac and I shared my whole time there. How we would look at each other and speak in a language only the abused know.

"You don't belong here."

"I know."

12

GOD, WHERE THE FUCK ARE YOU?

I sometimes wonder just where God is as I gaze out into the shattered roiling world we now find ourselves in. I have to often ask myself, Is this the way it's always been? Like, have people always been this petty and cruel and so perfectly disinterested in empathy for one another? Have people always been so quick to dismiss the entire lived experience of one another so casually?

History tells us yes. America's legacy is beyond brutal. I can only speak from my experience as a queer Black male who was born poor, but if we are to judge this country, its systems, and its people by the way it treats its most vulnerable, then by any measure of love, any measure of dignity, this country, and by proxy all of us, are without any hope of redemption. Take a look at what's been made plain since a global pandemic rocked our society and the global community: a designed disaster woven into the American dream with sharp edges meant to cut Black and brown bodies to ribbons while capitalists weather a tsunami of unnecessary death in relative comfort and ease. How can we see all this and not ask the question quite seriously, "God, where the fuck are you?"

Because if I was to just use the last decade as a measuring stick, we are coming up way short of hope. I have often called myself a post-Charleston preacher. Meaning the week that I started my formation as a church leader, the first week I put on a clerical collar to serve the people as someone pursuing ordination, was the week of the Charleston massacre. The only context in which I have had the role of proclaiming to my community about foolish hope and a salvation that overcomes even death, the only time in human history I have talked about a liberating God who is going to great lengths to bend the world to a place of equity, radical affirmation, and perhaps a spiritual revolution. A revolution given context by names like Mike Brown. Sandra Bland. Sandy Hook Elementary. I have preached to a backdrop of hate rallies led by an aging reality TV star like some dark noir comic book from the '80s where nuclear Armageddon is a bygone conclusion. I have only practiced ministry during the rough ride we have been on as a country right alongside Freddie Gray. So you would think that all the ecclesiastical red tape I have endured, the white supremacy I have found coiled around the heart of Christian theology, and the very real roadblocks and people who made it their mission to see that someone like me would never be ordained—or just the existential angst of the twenty-first century—would be enough to make me walk away from this whole God thing.

But there is another story that runs counter to the narrative that is playing out in the public square with surprising ferocity and increased damage to the national psyche. It is the gentle and surprising story of a grace-filled America that is building up all around us despite the systemic evil that we have called our institutions and our republic since their inception. A network of love and familial connections that touch communities across time and space, full of people who are the answer to the question "Is God real?" Their lives scream a resounding yes. The patterns in which they move throughout the world are the deep rhythms of life that are the very makeup of the Kin-dom of God. So even when I look upon the world, even when some red hat screams in my face that I have somehow made up a global pandemic as some sort of referendum of their sophomorically evil leader, I have hope.

Because of you, beloved.

Lived experience paints a different picture than the common morose despair we seem to be covered in lately. Because in between the headlines and the notifications flooding my phone telling me how fatally flawed human-ity is and my own growing cynicism, there is you. *And you are lovely.* I may not know you personally, but I know people like you who have wrestled with the sacred stories of others, who still seek God even though the institutional church tried its best to beat that instinct out of you. You who have suffered the thousand tiny cuts a community can inflict on you if you are queer or Black, Indigenous, or a person of color (BIPOC). You see, I don't know who is holding this book, but I know your spirit, I know your love, I know your prayers and energy, because they have been surrounding me my whole life. It is the same energy that knit my bones together in my mother's womb and made them queer and holy. You are the cloud of witnesses and angels I have encountered my whole life, disguised as the sweet kiss you gave me last Saturday night. Or the open door of a car that careens to a stop by the side of the road to pick up a thirteen-year-old boy with no road of his own to travel. Your prayers have been the tissue surrounding my beating heart. I know you were probably not praying, meditating, or out sowing goodness specifically for me. But I encountered it. I continue to encounter the raw, unmanipulated, multifaceted spark of divinity that the Creator has hidden inside each and every one of you.

That's how I finally heard it whispering from deep down inside of me too. By recognizing the beauty in you, I was finally able to see it in myself, but briefly, a moment, really, and that changed everything. That radically realigned the trajectory of my fate, and now my hope is that by sharing my story, you can see the beauty in me. And in yourself.

That by tracking down my path through this wild country full of contradictions, oppression, liberation, artists, farmers, hatemongers, peacemakers, and a thousand other binaries they try to put us all in, my hope is you can see clearly where I am coming from. With specificity. Particularity. With cultural authenticity and voice. With scars and mistakes plain to see. I hope you can hear me. Because it has been the greatest spiritual discovery of my life to listen to you. When I can hear you and figure out specifically where you are and where you are coming from, my role in this world, with this God, becomes clearer. It unfolds before me, and all seem aligned in harmony with the stars. When I get to know and love you, I suddenly exist in a world that runs right alongside the one I have always known. One that is inhabited with futures unmarred and real love and power here and now to set right a world that we all sense has gone horribly wrong.

This kind of love transcends so many of the petty divisions created by people of goodwill and threatens the power structures that cynically use the health care system as the latest weapon against the poor. Who, in the midst of a pandemic, have taken out the abacus of human consequence and weighed percentage points of the economy against the lives of your grandmother and my community. Who have stood at the very pinnacle of the temple of end-stage capitalist decadence and decay and made a very different choice than the man from Nazareth so many of them claim to worship. Crimes against human-ity sold to us a patriotic response to a crisis—I have to tell you that it isn't anything new. What has been made plain about those who rule us and their corporate mas-ters is the unsurprising response of evil when it discovers it cannot sustain itself on a suddenly unwilling popu-lation that has seen this thin and pale rider trek across this nation to the tune of hundreds of thousands of American lives at the time of writing this book.

What I mean is there is a death pact between our politi-cal structure and our economic overlords, and they will take us all with them with little to no forethought. COVID-19 has simply revealed not only the largely unrealized depths of depravity to which they are willing to go but also the thing that keeps me going most days. The great hope that COVID-19 has revealed in the midst of the charnel-house response from a White House—which has never been whiter—is just how completely vulnerable they are.

That's where God is in the midst of this. That's where the Holy One known as I am resides currently in our coun-try. God is the cracks, flaws, and splintering pillars of a system that can't support its own bloated weight. Think about it—we stayed home for two months, and the repub-lic almost collapsed.

Community didn't collapse. Mercy didn't collapse. Love for neighbor didn't fall in upon itself and scream like a petulant child onto the airwaves how its own inherent worth was so self-evident that everyone should be willing to risk their lives and those of the most vulnerable they love in its name. No, it was not the people who started that national conversation; it was those we have invested with incredible power who have long abandoned even a pretense of the grand dream of democracy and have functioned like most dying predators do when cornered. The thin veneer of the rule of law—long a joke to anyone not white in this country—has been scrapped by disaster. We are living through an unveiling, a revelation. Tearing off the mask of this strange creature we have allowed to live off our labor, love, art, family, lifeblood, sweat, and joy, we see its terrible visage and the dark abyss it has been beckoning us toward all along.

God is the "unveiler." We are the proof that love is on the move.

I can't help but think that it is at the fall of great empires when the very consciousness of humanity shifts and we are full up with infinite possibility. I mean, it seems to me that at important points in history, the divine seems to break in for the express cause of setting the world aright again, and not only that, but there are generations that are called to this task, whole nations of peoples, often in spite of their leaders.

We might be one of those nations of peoples. We might be one of those generations. This might well be one of those times in human history. *It feels like it.*

It feels like we are all standing cliffside shoulder to shoulder, overlooking the desert that is our country while a new day dawns. You see, there is hope by the edge in the desert. The people of God have always found hope in the desert. It's never been because an empire provided it. I think there is a well of living water to be found in this generation that can sate the thirst of this world. And I don't think I'm alone in this belief. I think there is a whole overly traumatized ragtag army of volunteers willing to risk it all to further the cause of love on earth one more time. To try our hand at grace once more. To believe in the sense of home we find in one another and the dream of a great society springing from that interconnectedness that we have always known to be so true but has become a matter of life and death.

What I am trying to tell you is that I have found God. God is hidden in the defiance in your eyes when you march. In the revulsion you feel when you see the prison-industrial complex for what it is. God is the transwomen I know who are in the South organizing and taking the heat for BIPOC siblings. God is the first whiff of a cup of coffee a weary volunteer smells on their way in to feed folks in their community. A community that through predatory economics and end-stage capitalism has been left behind while Wall Street bathes in their earnings. In that same community, God is the birthday in the park that is full of Black boy joy, balloons, and the ancestors. God is the decorations blowing in the wind and the little girl playing double Dutch who is the future senator for the district, though no one would guess that yet. God is the queer pastors who invested in me and helped me be me fully and holy. Or wholly, if you prefer. These rainbow-stole, glitter-infused theologians who taught me more about the true meaning of fidelity outside heteronormative paradigms than I will ever be able to share. They are where God is hiding. In their faithful hearts. There, weaved into the hope that someday the church would say yes to them, is the very makeup of the Holy Spirit. God is on a packed subway right now on their way to work with their kid they are dropping off to day care. Their only begotten son looks up at them with perfect love as they walk off at Broadway Junction to get on the C train. God is a Black woman on her way to work weaving through the crowds on a subway platform in Brooklyn hoping to make the same connections we are. Hoping to make it home on time. Her son gripping her hand in perfect trust and love.

Once you start looking for hope, you find out that it's everywhere. Once you start to notice the patterns of mercy etched into the very foundations of the world, you will never unsee them. Once you find grace stuffed into the margins of your story, you can't help but drag it out for all to see. Because we may have a long battle for the soul of this country still ahead, but God is present in this struggle. God is the struggle. God is the friend who winks and hands you a bandanna and a water bottle full of white stuff just as the tear gas lands near your feet.

Amen.

EPILOGUE

Today

I write to you from a tiny home I rented in Forks, Washington. Its 7:23 a.m., and I have received two phone calls for comment from the media in the last twenty-four hours and one at 6 a.m. from a persistent Russian news network I gave comment to once. Suddenly I am their Black church expert. Or their racism expert. I can't remember what I said to them two years prior, but they always call me—something about the president jerking off to racist fever dreams in the White House. The reporter I usually deal with calls and just starts reciting Black trauma into the phone that woke me from my sleep. I listen as she speaks death over my people, destruction over my community, and pestilence on the land. She is just reporting the facts. I hang up as she recites the president's latest comments to me and listen to my phone buzz for fifteen minutes.

It's May 29, 2020, and the smoke is still rising over parts of Minneapolis, Minnesota, this morning. Bree, my partner and wife, and a lot of my friends are starting to become really concerned about my emotional and spiritual health. I am on the ragged edge. The year prior was nonstop: I just completed a book tour for my first work, *Dear Church: A Love Letter from a Black Preacher to the Whitest Denomination in the US*, and have spent the last year working at least forty hours a week at the church I was serving in Brooklyn while crisscrossing the country talking about systemic racism in the church. I had been to almost every region in my denomination and in this country preparing us with everything I had for a moment like this. Like the one unfolding in front of a captive audience during quarantine from the streets of Minneapolis. The macabre opera that is white supremacy in America, with its piercing falsetto shattering the thin veneer of civilization white America happily cast away at a moment's notice in its lust to gorge itself on Black blood. And I am tired.

So we came to hide me in the woods from Black trauma. It isn't working. I have been peppered with it all morning. I am supposed to be tying in a neat little bow on this book for you, the whole point of this story. That hope, grace, and mercy are still alive and well in this country.

I succumb to the text messages and open Twitter. I watch as a Black reporter from CNN is arrested while live on the air—he was Black and was covering the state troopers as they moved into the area of uprising in the Twin Cities. I read a tweet from the sitting president of the United States suggesting the best way to deal with Black folk when they are riled up is to gun them down. He suggests that police start shooting us.

It's not yet 9 a.m. PST. I'm looking at flights to the Twin Cities and dreading the conversation with Bree when she wakes up. I had told her last night I was praying about going. The news this morning won't sell her on me getting on a plane to a city I may not come back from. I have several felonies, black skin, and a loud mouth. We make decisions like this as a family. My daughter is usually the veto vote. Do we have enough bail money? Do we know lawyers there, not a friend of a friend, who do we know? Is the bishop of the territory known for racial justice work? The risks are higher for me and my family to engage in direct action, and it means I often sit on the sidelines to witness and write. I preach or teach about the battle for my very personhood, but if I get one or two more felonies in the pursuit of freedom, they could build a case to put me away for years, while my white peers are released from a protest with a fine.

This has become untenable to me. I have started to chafe at the role of witness God has placed me in the last decade, and it's starting to kill me. I can't see any more death or destruction. *Strife and turmoil lay before me, and the law has become slack.*

Hope, grace, and mercy. A vision of a United States of Grace.

Everyone, when they look back on this story over the next few years, will tell you about the police station that protesters overran, reclaimed, or liberated, depending on your perspective or just how much this country has kicked your ass. They will tell you that was the big story. I want to tell you about a little Lutheran church right by the Target—you know which Target, the one that caused so much anguish in white America as it burned near the murder scene of George Floyd.

Holy Trinity Lutheran Church. I have never been, but I have never wanted to go more than I do the day I write this. The pastors' names are Ingrid and Angela, and they have no idea I am writing this, nor will they until publication. You see, while the rest of America sheds crocodile tears for a Target and a police station being laid to ruin, Holy Trinity came to life. The empire wept over its capitalist toy being broken on TV in front of those still in its thrall; they gnashed their teeth and threw ashes on their heads that the centurions at the police station might be inconvenienced for a few weeks because of the fire. But right next door, the Kin-dom of God sprang into life and resurrection.

Holy Trinity provided sanctuary and medical care to frontline freedom fighters. They started becoming a hub and way station for information. Soon every resource folks who serve in my tradition could muster was brought to bear on this community, but I'm sure they will pay the much larger cost in ways none of us will be able to measure for years to come. Because white supremacy always retaliates against those who succeed (even briefly, even in small ways) in the fight for liberation.

They became, briefly, chaplains to the revolution. Honestly, is there ever a better job for the church? As a church leader, I can tell you the last thing this country needs is the church in charge of anything. But a church that moves toward human suffering in solidarity with all the ways the divine expresses itself across cultures and social location, a church willing to walk on Lake Street in Minneapolis and call out through the tear gas, "Hey, over here! Over here, you can find sanctuary." That's a church worth living and dying for.

That's a country worth living and dying for. Not the strip mall and its destruction or the bootjacks of racist policy structures the police have become in America. The communities that call out in solidarity to those experiencing oppression. The people who step out onto the street and are willing to bleed for those they love, to die for their community. That's who we are at our core and why I love this country so much.

The cunning thing about America is that the very fabric of it could be either the protesters or the police for you.

God bless those who are waging peace in the battle for the soul of America. The words they call out are the sacred scripture of liberation and freedom that is written into every human heart.

The Kin-dom of God was near Lake Street in Minneapolis today. One of its closest vineyards was Holy Trinity Lutheran Church. The two stewards who tended that vineyard couldn't be more different. One a Black woman leader in the whitest denomination in America. The other born, bred, and raised in its white heritage. "Lutheranism," disguised as a false immigrant culture that abdicated its responsibility when it became the majority culture, enjoyed so much privilege as a result. Both working and serving together.

Hope, grace, and mercy. A vision of a United States of Grace.

I write to you now when I can't even stand within six feet of you. I have written a large portion of this book in quarantine while the reckless destruction of Black bodies laid bare by this pandemic is on display before me. Before you.

I'm in Forks, Washington, as far as I can get—within the continental United States—from most of the country, and I'm starting to realize that a mask and six feet of social distance may not be enough to survive you, America.

And I still believe in you because I am left with no other choice. I am heir to the republic I built, but you deny me, sibling in a struggle of your creation and fellow worker of the grand vision of what we could be if we but believed in our own fucking promises.

I am American. I am as American as apple pie, slavery, and extrajudicial killings. I am as American as beat poets, soul music, and protests. I am as American as Mount Rainier, which I can see in the distance this morning, and Lake Street in Minneapolis.

Lake Street is Main Street America, and that's where I live. It's where I may die. It's where I write to you today about a United States of Grace.

I don't know where this book will find you or us as a country.

But I do know the forces of love always find each other and gather. I know that love wins.

> In the name of the Parent,
> the Rebel, and the Spirit,
>
> The Rev. Lenny Duncan ✠

ACKNOWLEDGMENTS

It's impossible to thank everyone who helps shape a book. I believe you are sent a team of souls by the Creator and the ancestors as you give birth to *your* sacred story. There are so many faces and people and so much love that goes into a book. All are family. My family knows they are family. We know the *real ones*. You know if you are a real one to me or not. **Thank you.** It has always seemed silly to me when a writer thanked a loving Creator for that Creator's grace and mercy. If I am right on this rather strange premise about the universe—that this Power is real and at work in the world—that Creator knows my deep and abiding gratitude. If some of you are right, then I am writing and talking to nothing and no one. *But I wanted to take note of how much Grace I have been given, none of which I ever had to earn.* I feel it's very on-brand for this book to acknowledge the inexplicable and unexplainable and fall short of describing it in terms that satisfy me and for sure will frustrate you, the reader. Finally, my editor, Lisa Kloskin. She is dope. If you have this book in your hand, I hope we both are grateful for her work by the end.

This is a sincere and humble submission to the great canon of Black stories of liberation, joy, survival, and (I still hope) salvation in this republic. I have with all honesty and forthrightness tried to use my Black story, its proximity to whiteness, my trauma, my gifts, my talents, my treasures, and all the broken pieces of my life as an offering on the altar of our collective freedom. I give all that I am, or was, or ever could be forever to this joint task of righting a weary and troubled world. I believe the most precious thing we can give, that we often give too freely, is our own story. This is my contribution. My entire life.

Written in Liberation and Love,
Lenny Duncan